TORPEDOED

TORPEDOED

THE TRUE STORY OF THE
WORLD WAR II
SINKING OF "THE CHILDREN'S SHIP"

DEBORAH HEILIGMAN

GODWINBOOKS

HENRY HOLT AND COMPANY
New York

Henry Holt and Company, *Publishers since 1866*
Henry Holt® is a registered trademark of Macmillan Publishing Group, LLC
120 Broadway, New York, New York 10271 • mackids.com

Permission to use the following images is gratefully acknowledged:
i–iii, 10: Shutterstock; 42–43: University of Glasgow Archives, photograph by author;
200: Imperial War Museum, photograph by author. Additional credits are noted with captions.

Library of Congress Cataloging-in-Publication Data
Names: Heiligman, Deborah, author.
Title: Torpedoed : the true story of the World War II sinking of
"The Children's Ship" / Deborah Heiligman.
Other titles: True story of the World War II sinking of "The Children's Ship"
Description: New York : Godwin Books, Henry Holt and Company, [2019] |
Includes bibliographical references and index. | Audience: Ages 10–14.
Identifiers: LCCN 2019002536 | ISBN 9781627795548 (hardcover)
Subjects: LCSH: City of Benares (Ship)—Juvenile literature. | World War, 1939–1945—
Children—Great Britain—Juvenile literature. | World War, 1939–1945—Evacuation of
civilians—Great Britain—Juvenile literature. | World War, 1939–1945—Naval operations,
German—Juvenile literature. | Shipwrecks—North Atlantic Ocean—Juvenile literature. |
World War, 1939–1945—Personal narratives, British—Juvenile literature.
Classification: LCC D772.C46 H45 2018 | DDC 940.54/293—dc23
LC record available at https://lccn.loc.gov/2019002536

Our books may be purchased in bulk for promotional, educational, or business use.
Please contact your local bookseller or the Macmillan Corporate and Premium
Sales Department at (800) 221-7945 ext. 5442 or by email at
MacmillanSpecialMarkets@macmillan.com.

First edition, 2019 / Designed by Raphael Geroni
Printed in the United States of America by LSC Communications, Harrisonburg, Virginia
1 3 5 7 9 10 8 6 4 2

FOR JOHN BAKER,

FOR SONIA WILLIAMS,

——— *and* ———

IN MEMORY OF ALL THOSE

WHO DIED

CONTENTS

A NOTE TO READERS

The Red Jacket

A few years ago, my editor showed me a photograph of a custom-made child's life jacket. Do you want to look into this story, she asked? I did! And what a story it turned out to be—one full of drama and despair, triumph and joy. It's a story of people who become heroes and of innocents who die. A tale of people who survive against the odds.

It is a true story. There is nothing made up in this book.

When recalling an event that happened so long ago, people who were there can have different memories. When people go through a traumatic event, they remember important details, but some things get lost or misremembered. I have reconstructed the events as best I could, relying on memories of the survivors both close to the event and decades later.

You will notice that most of the dialogue is not set in quotation marks. I used quotation marks for material that came from a letter or journal written at or close to that time. A lot of the dialogue comes from interviews decades later. People don't tend to remember *exactly* what was said. But they do remember the gist of it. I wanted to use the dialogue they remembered, but I felt more comfortable omitting quotation marks around it.

You will also notice that I have included very few names and personal stories of the sailors from India, called lascars, even though they made up most of the crew. Because of racism and classism, nobody interviewed the lascars at the time. I tried to find survivors and relatives of survivors so I could include their memories, but even with the help of people in India and England, I could not find anyone. That said, we know they were there. We know they, too, were heroes, and that many of them died.

This is a story of war. I hope telling it will lead to less war and more peace.

Opposite: *Colin Ryder Richardson's life jacket.* [Sarah Ryder Richardson, courtesy of the Egham Museum]

SHIPMATES

On the *City of Benares*

Patricia Allen, 12, CORB child, also a passenger on *Volendam*

John (Johnny) Baker, 7, CORB child

Robert (Bobby) Baker, 12, CORB child

Barbara Bech, 15, traveling with her mother and siblings

Derek Bech, 9

Marguerite Bech, mother of the Bech children

Sonia Bech, 11

Michael Brooker, 10, CORB child, also a passenger on *Volendam*

Patricia (Pat) Bulmer, 14, traveling with her mother

Ramjam Buxoo, crew member, Lifeboat 12

Alan Capel, 5, CORB child

Derek Capel, 12, CORB child, Lifeboat 12

Howard Claytor, 11, CORB child, Lifeboat 12

Ronald (Ronnie) Cooper, fourth officer of *City of Benares*, captain of Lifeboat 12

Mary Cornish, 41, music teacher, CORB escort, Lifeboat 12

George Crawford, 13, CORB child

Doug Critchley, sea cadet on the *City of Benares*, Lifeboat 12

Elizabeth (Beth) Cummings, 14, CORB child

Eric Davis, BBC reporter, on raft with Jack Keely

Marjorie Day, head CORB escort

Maureen Dixon, 10, CORB child

Sybil Gilliat-Smith, 25, artist, CORB escort

Ruby Grierson, filmmaker making a documentary about CORB children

Augusta (Gussie) Grimmond, 13, CORB child

Connie Grimmond, 9, CORB child

Edward Jr. (Eddie) Grimmond, 8, CORB child

Leonard (Lennie) Grimmond, 5, CORB child

Violet, Grimmond, 10, CORB child

Terrence Holmes, 10, CORB child

Joan Irving, 15, CORB child

Jack Keeley, 9, CORB child

Joyce Keeley, 6, CORB child

Edmond Mackinnon, admiral, commodore of the convoy

Johnny Mayhew, Royal Navy signaler on *City of Benares*, Lifeboat 12

John McGlashan, second engineer of the *City of Benares*, on raft with Jack Keeley

Tommy Milligan, crew member of the *City of Benares*, on raft with the Bechs

Ailsa Murphy, 10, CORB child

Beryl Myatt, 9, CORB child

Bohdan Nagorski, Polish businessman and passenger, Lifeboat 12

Landles Nicoll, captain of the
City of Benares

Father Roderic (Rory) O'Sullivan,
priest, CORB escort, Lifeboat 12

Harry Peard, gunner on the
City of Benares, Lifeboat 12

George Purvis, assistant steward
of the *City of Benares*, Lifeboat 12

Laszlo Raskai, Hungarian BBC
journalist, Colin's chaperone

Michael Rennie, 23, CORB escort

Colin Ryder Richardson, 11,
traveling alone

Paul Shearing, 11, CORB child,
Lifeboat 12

William (Bill) Short, 9,
CORB child, Lifeboat 12

Peter Short, 5, CORB child

Kenneth (Ken) Sparks, 12,
CORB child, Lifeboat 12

Rosemary Spencer-Davies, 15,
CORB child

Harry Frederick (Fred) Steels, 11,
CORB child, Lifeboat 12

Abdul Subhan, crew member

Rex Thorne, 13, CORB child

Marion (Mary) Thorne, 7,
CORB child

Lilian Towns, CORB escort

Bess Walder, 15, CORB child

Louis Walder, 10, CORB child

Doris Walker, passenger en route
to Australia, on raft with
the Bechs

Ann Watson, 6, CORB child

Arthur Wimperis, 66, English
playwright, screenwriter en
route to Hollywood

Eleanor Wright, 13, CORB child

Margaret Zeal, CORB doctor

CORB officials

Elsbeth Davies, CORB welfare
director

Geoffrey Shakespeare, head of the
CORB program

On the *Hurricane*

Peter Collinson, doctor

Patrick Fletcher, navigator

Albert Gorman, skipper of the
Hurricane's whaler

Hugh Crofton Simms, captain

On U-Boat 48

Heinrich "Ajax" Bleichrodt,
Kapitänleutnant commander

Rolf Hilse, wireless radio engineer

Others

Mr. and Mrs. Baker, Bobby and
Johnny's parents

Alan Francis, 10, child from
Wembley, not in CORB

Edward (Eddie) and Hannah
Grimmond, parents of five
CORB children

Eileen Paterson,
Mary Cornish's sister

Ian Paterson, Eileen's husband,
Mary Cornish's brother-in-law

Leslie Lewis, skipper of the
Marina lifeboat

Mr. and Mrs. Walder, Bess and
Louis's parents

CHAPTER 1

The Noise of War

SEPTEMBER 17, 1940, NIGHTTIME

IN THE MID-ATLANTIC Ocean, a German war submarine has an ocean liner in its sights. The U-boat commander and his crew have been following the ship all day. They are waiting for the right moment.

The two hundred passengers on the ship have no idea a U-boat lurks beneath the water, ready to attack. One hundred of the passengers are children. Most of them are in bed, asleep in their pajamas.

A few minutes before 10 p.m., the commander of U-boat 48 gives the order: Torpedoes away—

EIGHT DAYS EARLIER

IN LONDON, THE AIR RAID SIGNAL SOUNDED.

Another night of bombing. Gussie Grimmond, thirteen, and her family rushed from their house to their underground shelter. As the bombs exploded in the night sky, raining down on the city, Gussie huddled with her parents and her nine brothers and sisters. Even underground she could hear the noise of war: air raid sirens wailing; bombs exploding; terrifying bangs, whistles, and shrieks echoing through the city. The ground shook, too. The Grimmonds were safe for now, but war was all around them.

A German Heinkel He 111 bomber flies over
England at the start of the Blitz, September 7, 1940.
[Wikimedia Commons/Australian War Memorial]

It was September 9, 1940. On September 7, a sunny Saturday afternoon, Germans had begun bombing London, pummeling it for hours. The bombing did not stop completely until four thirty the next morning. By the end of that first day and night of bombing, more than four hundred people had died—including children. Many more children and adults were injured.

It was one year into World War II. The United States wasn't fighting with Britain against Germany—yet. And for most of the past year, the battles had stayed away from British shores, too. But this summer the war had become real for the British people, like Gussie and her family. The Germans had started bombing *them*.

At first the Germans bombed only military targets, trying to destroy Royal Air Force planes, aircraft factories, and coastal radar stations. RAF pilots fought back, battling in the skies above.

Pilots from all over the world signed up to fight with Britain. These two Polish RAF pilots play with their squadron's mascot, a puppy.
[Imperial War Museum]

The Brits kept count of how many German planes were shot down, cheering on the Royal Air Force. The RAF pilots were already heroes. As Prime Minister Winston Churchill declared, "Never in the field of human conflict was so much owed by so many to so few."

Now the Germans were bombing not only air bases but also civilians in London, the port city of Liverpool, and other English towns. Bombs demolished office buildings, schools, playgrounds, churches, and houses. *Homes*. Ordinary citizens like Gussie and her sisters and brothers were in mortal danger. This was the third night in a row that the Grimmonds had to spend underground.

When would it end? How many more nights would Gussie and her family have to huddle together like this, fearing for their home and their lives?

And it would probably get worse. Adolf Hitler, Nazi Germany's dictator, threatened to invade by land. The British had every reason to believe that Hitler would follow through with this threat and send his army across the English Channel. This Blitz on London was part of his blitzkrieg, or lightning war. After taking over Austria and Czechoslovakia, Hitler had used blitzkrieg tactics to invade Poland in 1939, and German tanks had since rolled across Europe. Tens of thousands of soldiers *and* civilians already had died as Hitler seized Denmark, Norway, Belgium, the Netherlands, Luxembourg, and France. Hitler was determined to add Britain to the list. He wanted to take over the world.

Winston Churchill refused to give in to German force. In his first speech as prime minister, just four months earlier, Churchill had vowed "to wage war, by sea, land and air, with all our might and with all the strength that God can give us; to wage war against a monstrous tyranny never surpassed in the dark, lamentable catalogue of human crime."

The British government insisted its citizens take safety measures. There was a universal blackout across the country every night, with shades blocking all indoor light, so that German planes would not be guided to their targets. And when the air raid siren sounded its up-and-down notes, signaling an attack about to begin, all civilians had to hurry underground to safety, as Gussie and her family had. Only air raid wardens and emergency workers were supposed to be outside during the bombing raids.

Devastation caused by Nazi air raids on Westminster, London, with the houses of Parliament and the clock tower with the famous bell, Big Ben, still standing. [Mary Evans Picture Library]

The wardens instructed people to move calmly but quickly to neigh-borhood shelters, underground subway stations, or their basements if they couldn't get anywhere else. To stay in your living room or bed-room was to put your life in peril. Some families, like the Grimmonds, had their own shelters, issued by the government. The Grimmonds had managed to add on to their Anderson shelter—made of corrugated steel—to make room for their large family.

All that night, as Gussie and her family stayed safely underground, London's streets were dangerous and chaotic. Buildings toppled from the bombs. Explosions ignited fires, shooting red-orange flames into the darkness and spreading from one building to the next, destroying even more lives.

Firefighters and medics drove their fire trucks and ambulances as best they could through dark, rubble-strewn streets. Firefighters quickly unfurled hoses to douse fires. They rushed into buildings

Winston Churchill speaks to his nation on BBC radio in 1940.
[Mary Evans Picture Library]

to rescue people trapped by flames and searched through rubble, hoping to save people buried under collapsed buildings. Rescuers put their own lives in danger trying to save others, and yet on they worked—men too old to fight in the war, others not yet called up; women driving ambulances and fire trucks, working as fire watchers, medics, nurses.

In the morning, when the Germans stopped bombing, the all-clear signal sounded. It was one long continuous note, a slightly off C-sharp. Everyone knew that note meant it was safe to come out. People all over London emerged from their shelters. Most went back to their homes to have breakfast and start their days. But some were not so lucky.

When the Grimmonds climbed out, exhausted from too little sleep, they did not see their house. What they saw instead was a

Firefighters hose the still-burning remains of bombed buildings in London. [Mary Evans Picture Library]

pile of rubble. Everything they owned was destroyed—furniture, clothing, toys, dishes. All of it, gone. Had they stayed in their home, they would have died.

Among their destroyed belongings were five packed suitcases. Gussie and her younger sisters, Violet, ten, and Connie, nine, and two of her little brothers, Eddie, eight, and Lennie, five, were on the waiting list for a journey that would get them out of England to safety. These five Grimmond children were scheduled to go to Liverpool that very day. If they were lucky enough to get off the waiting list, Gussie and her brothers and sisters would board a ship for Canada, part of a government program called the Children's Overseas Reception Board. The CORB program required that children be no younger than five and no older than fifteen. There was room for ninety CORB children on the ship.

Gussie's parents, Eddie and Hannah Grimmond, looked at the pile of rubble. Hannah held her youngest, a toddler, in her arms and argued with her husband. She did not see how she could let Gussie, Violet, Connie, Eddie Jr., and Lennie go on the journey without the clothes, shoes, towels, food—everything they had been told to pack. But her husband, Eddie, was sure the people from CORB would help outfit the children if they got off the waiting list. It was worth the chance. The rest of the family had to go live in temporary housing, anyway, with nothing of their own. Why not give these five the opportunity to escape across the ocean?

Eddie Grimmond had fought in the First World War, and he knew personally the horrors of war. His best friend had died. When the war was over, he went to visit his buddy's widow, Hannah. They married and had a family, ten children in all. They were very close, the whole large brood, but now five might be able to escape to safety. How could they not try to get them out? It was easy to see that side of the argument. They were homeless. And it clearly was not safe in London.

The Grimmonds could send Gussie, Violet, Connie, Eddie, and Lennie. Although it seemed like a great opportunity, it was very difficult for Hannah to let any of her children go the day after her home was destroyed. And of course there was danger at sea—U-boats were already torpedoing ships in the Atlantic Ocean. In fact, U-boat 48 had departed its home port of Lorient, France, two days earlier, with two minesweeper escorts. At 9:45, after guiding the submarine safely out, the escorts left, their lights flashing, wishing the crew good luck and good hunting.

Hannah didn't know this, of course, and she didn't know whether her children would even be allowed on the CORB ship. But she agreed it was worth the chance. Eddie would take the children to the station and put them on a train to Liverpool. In Liverpool their safety would be up to the CORB people, and fate.

As she said goodbye to her children, Hannah had no idea how long it would be until she saw them again. If they were allowed onto the ship, she might not see them until the war was over, which could be months, as people hoped, but more likely *years*. The previous war had lasted more than four years. For Hannah Grimmond, it would turn out to be much worse than that.

....

WHEN EDDIE AND his children arrived at London's Euston Station, the platform was filled with parents sending their children away. There were promises and instructions as CORB children and parents said goodbye, hugging, kissing, crying. One of the older children leaving for Liverpool later described it as an emotionally charged opera.

ICELAND

ATLANTIC OCEAN

N
W   E
S

SCOTLAND
Glasgow

Escort ships depart

NORTHERN
IRELAND

City of Benares sinks

Dublin

IRELAND

Liverpool

ENGLAND
London

BELGIUM

The Course of the
SS *CITY of BENARES*
(September 13–17, 1940)

FRANCE

But Gussie and her brothers and sisters were in a kind of stupor, drained from the long nights in the underground shelter and dazed from the shock of seeing the rubble that used to be their home. They said goodbye to their father and got on the train.

Gussie was in the middle of the family at home, but she was the oldest of these five, and she easily stepped into the role of big sister. She made sure her two sisters and two brothers all sat quietly and didn't run around the train. They arrived in Liverpool in a couple of hours, all together and more or less ready for their trip—assuming they could get on the ship.

If there was any place to start an adventure, especially a dangerous one, it was this city. Set on the Irish Sea along the river Mersey, Liverpool had a reputation, history, and atmosphere of danger. The air was misty and foggy, the land marshy. There was

Above: *CORB children and their escorts on the way to New Zealand.* [The National Archives UK] • Opposite: *The route of the SS City of Benares.* [Raphael Geroni]

even quicksand! A century earlier, the streets and alleys had teemed with ruffians and smugglers. Privateers and pirates preyed on passing ships.

Now, in 1940, the most serious danger came from German bombers above. Would the port of Liverpool—essential to the war effort—survive?

High atop a building sat two stone birds, imaginary Liver Birds. (*Liver* rhymes with *diver*.) They say the male Liver Bird faces inward, to the city, to see if pubs are open, reflecting Liverpool's sense of humor and fun. But the female Liver Bird faces outward, toward the docks, waiting solemnly for sailors to return home safely.

Port cities are doorways to the world, but they are also vulnerable to attack. Liverpudlians say that if the Liver Birds ever fly away, Liverpool will cease to exist.

....

THE CORB CHILDREN did not stay near the docks, which were targets of German night bombing. Gussie and the other CORB children were taken to the Sherwood's Lane School, a bit outside the city center, to stay for a couple of nights. At the school, the children would meet their chaperones and the other children in their groups.

When the CORB officials learned that the Grimmond house had been destroyed, they took Gussie and her sisters and brothers off the reserve list and, just as their father had hoped, gave them everything they needed. The boys, Eddie and Lennie, were put in a group of boys with a male chaperone; Gussie, Connie, and Violet in a group of girls, with a woman.

Gussie made a great impression on the adults immediately. She was quite thin, all bones and angles, and her face looked pinched and worn. But she was very strong, strong-willed, smart, funny, and quirky. Once the Grimmonds were accepted into the program, she showed she was eager to please the adults. The Sherwood's Lane headmistress later remarked that Gussie could summon up quite a bit of Cockney bossiness to keep her sisters and brothers in line.

Back in London, Hannah and Eddie settled themselves and the rest of the family into a homeless shelter until they could find other housing. The Grimmonds were now split in half. In a few days a ship would leave Liverpool, and Gussie, Violet, Connie, Eddie, and Lennie Grimmond would be on it. If all went as planned, those five Grimmond children would live out the war in safety.

Even if all did not go as expected, there was no way now to undo the decision Hannah and Eddie had made.

CHAPTER 2

Sailing to Safety

IT HAD BEEN a hot September so far, but Thursday, September 12, 1940, was a cool day in Liverpool, where Gussie, Violet, and Connie Grimmond waited with their group at the busy docks to board the ship. Seagulls squawked overhead as waves from the river Mersey lapped against the shore. Liverpool was a gateway to the British Empire from all over the world, and a departure point to the rest of the world from England. And at this moment, it was the passage to safety for the CORB group and the other passengers waiting to begin this journey.

Mary Cornish, a forty-one-year-old music teacher from London, stood with the Grimmond sisters and twelve other girls as they waited to embark. She was their chaperone, having volunteered for the job before her school year started. The girls in her group already loved her and called her Auntie Mary.

Ninety CORB children waited to board, six groups of fifteen children, each escorted by a chaperone. Before they left the school to board the ship, each child was given one last medical examination. Anyone who was sick (with chicken pox, for example) was sent back home.

There was a head escort, plus an extra chaperone, as well as a doctor and nurse, both women. Eddie and Lennie Grimmond were with their group of boys somewhere in the crowd. The ship they were all waiting to board was the *City of Benares*, though the name had been covered when the ship was repainted grey to make it less noticeable to German U-boats. The goal was to keep it safe—in case the Germans were looking to torpedo specific ships. The children wouldn't know the ship's name until they were on board and saw it on the lifeboats.

THERE WERE SO many children waiting to board. Among the CORB children, Bess Walder, fifteen, was one of the oldest. Like all the others, her parents had applied for her and her brother, Louis, ten, to be part of the program. When the children were accepted, they were not told when they would be leaving, or how, or from where. They had to wait for another letter with instructions, which would come right before the departure date.

SS City of Benares. [Imperial War Museum]

But as soon as they found out they'd been accepted into the program, Bess and Louis had started to pack. Their father brought down two trunks from the attic—large trunks—and the Walders packed them full of clothes and toys and books. Louis had packed his entire Hornby train set. Bess had packed all her favorite books and lots of knickknacks that were precious to her.

But when the next letter came, they discovered that CORB had a very specific packing list, which restricted them to a lot less: it included a gas mask, shirts, pants, pajamas, a sweater, a cap, shoes or boots, towels, six handkerchiefs, an ID card, a ration card, stationery and a pencil, and a Bible. No other books or toys were listed. Girls were supposed to bring a sewing kit. All the clothes had to be marked with names in indelible ink. And it all had to fit in a small suitcase—about twenty-six by eighteen inches.

Each child was also supposed to carry a sufficient supply of food and thirst-quenching fruit to last twenty-four hours. No glass bottles were allowed, but it would be good for each child to have a carton filled with either milk or water. They should pack sandwiches of egg and cheese. Other good foods to bring: packets of nuts and raisins, apples, bananas, oranges. They could pack barley-sugar candy, but not chocolate, and some biscuits (cookies) would be a good idea.

Mums and dads and children read over the list, used their ration coupons to buy what they needed, and got everything ready quickly, since they did not know when they would be called to leave. Parents also had to sign a permission slip and a disclaimer—because it was a dangerous trip.

The Walders unpacked the trunks and stowed them back in the attic. They packed two small suitcases instead. Louis took only the engine from his train set; Bess, a couple of books.

Opposite: *A CORB packing list.* [Imperial War Museum, photo by author]

CHILDREN'S OVERSEAS RECEPTION BOARD,

45, Berkeley Street,
LONDON, W.1.

The following is a suggested outfit for each child undertaking the journey:-

BOYS.	GIRLS

BOYS.

Gas Mask
1 Overcoat and mackintosh if possible
1 suit
1 pullover
1 hat or school cap.
2 shirts (coloured).
2 pairs stockings
2 undervests.
2 pairs pants
+ 2 pairs pyjamas
1 pair boots or shoes.
1 pair plimsolls
+ 6 handkerchiefs
+ 1 comb
+ 1 toothbrush and paste.
+ 1 face flannel
+ 1 towel
x 1 suitcase - about 26"x 18"
Stationery and pencil.
+ Ration card.
+ Identity card.
+ Birth Certificate (if possible)
Bible or New Testament.

1 attache case or haversack in which should be packed one of each of the items marked +

GIRLS

Gas Mask
1 Warm coat and mackintosh if possible.
1 cardigan or woollen jumper.
1 hat or beret.
1 pair warm gloves.
1 warm dress or skirt and jumper
2 pairs stockings
1 change of underclothing, including vests, knickers etc.
1 pair strong boots or shoes
1 pair plimsolls
2 cotton dresses or overalls with knickers.
+2 pairs pyjamas
+1 towel
+6 handkerchiefs
+1 hairbrush and comb.
+1 toothbrush and paste
+1 face flannel or sponge
+Sanitary towels
1 linen bag.
x 1 suitcase - about 26" x 18"
Sewing outfit
Stationery and pencil
+Ration card.
+Identity card.
+Birth Certificate (if possible)
Bible or New Testament.
1 Attache case or haversack in which should be packed one of each of the items marked +

x No trunk will be permitted.

All clothing should be clearly marked in indelible ink with the child's name.

No Passport will be required.

Each child should carry a sufficient supply of food and thirst quenching fruit to last 12 hours. It is particularly requested that no bottles should be carried, though it would be very desirable for each child to take a carton (½ pint) filled with either milk or water. The following are suitable and can easily be packed:-

=.Sandwiches, egg and cheese.
Packets of nuts and seedless raisins.
Dry biscuits and packets of cheese.
Barley sugar (not chocolate)
Apples, bananas, oranges.

=.Not more than two sandwiches, each of full loaf size, should be included.

All the CORB children and their parents were forbidden to tell anyone that they were going away. They were not supposed to talk about the program at all. "Loose lips sink ships," declared posters all over England. The enemy must not know when or where ships were sailing or what their cargo was or who the passengers were. In wartime England, you never knew who might be a spy.

Some of the CORB children didn't even know where they would be going. Many were heading off to stay with relatives, but some would live with strangers who had volunteered to take care of them. All the CORB children went to one of the faraway British dominions: Australia, New Zealand, South Africa, or Canada. (The United States was taking in children, too, but in a separate program.)

This group of CORB children was going to Canada. Bess and Louis were going to live with an aunt. They had been hearing about the war from their father. Mr. Walder had traveled a lot in Europe and for years had been worried about Adolf Hitler; he had seen a war coming.

A year earlier, at eleven o'clock in the morning, Britain had declared war on Germany. During the announcement, Bess and Louis had been in the street helping their father fill sandbags for fortifications in case the Germans invaded. And since the Blitz had begun, the Walder family slept every night in the shelter under the school where Mr. Walder was the caretaker. He was an air raid warden, too, and Mrs. Walder was in the Women's Voluntary Services, helping people who had been bombed out. When Bess heard about the CORB program, she asked to go. It took some persuading, but now here she was, and she was excited for the adventure.

When Bess had said goodbye to her father at the train station in London, he'd said to her—not for the first time—Watch after that young man. Meaning Louis, her little brother.

But since they'd arrived at Sherwood's Lane School, she had hardly seen Louis. He was in a separate boys' group, so she couldn't take care of him. She was actually relieved. Louis had been weak and sickly as a little boy, but now he was completely healthy—and a real handful.

Her mother's goodbye had been more puzzling. She'd said, Grow up to be a good woman.

Why would her mother say that? Wouldn't she see her soon? Her mother didn't seem upset, but that was a strange comment. Bess's parents, unlike many of the others, did not cry when they said goodbye. They were reserved, as was Bess.

Bess didn't know it, but when they left their children at the train station, Mrs. Walder was so shaken that she told her husband she needed a drink, badly. Mrs. Walder didn't usually drink alcohol, but her husband took her to a hotel bar so she could have a cocktail.

. . . .

JACK KEELEY WAS another of the CORB children. He had turned nine two months earlier and lived in a council apartment not far from Gussie and her family. Like all the CORB children, he carried a small suitcase and a gas mask, and he had his CORB identification disc on a bootlace around his neck. Jack was excited. Not only had he never been on a ship before, but he'd only left London once, for half a day. He and his family didn't have enough money to take trips or vacations.

Already this journey had been an adventure. His parents had taken him and his little sister, Joyce, six, to Euston Station. Jack's mum had told him to take care of Joyce. She was one of the youngest CORB children, and unlike Jack, Joyce was not excited at all, quite the opposite. She was very sad and kept crying, asking to go back home to her mother.

It was not unusual for some children to be homesick, and so the CORB adults had ways of helping them—sometimes with kindness and sometimes with toughness. The head of the CORB program, Geoffrey Shakespeare, tried to talk to all the CORB groups before they left. He told them to be strong, stoic, and British. "When things go wrong, as they often will," he said, "remember you are British and grin and bear it."

On an earlier CORB trip, after the children had arrived in Canada, one of the littler girls was crying. Echoing Mr. Shakespeare, an eleven-year-old told her, "Stop it at once and be British." The girl did.

Most of the homesick children felt better once the excitement took over. Not Joyce Keeley. She did not have fantasies about this kind of adventure, and she was too young to understand why she had to leave her mother. But Jack understood. He'd seen the newsreels before the cartoons at the tuppenny rush, the children's matinee movie on Saturdays. And he'd noticed the signs of war everywhere: lorries (trucks) with soldiers in the back, their guns pointed skyward, ready to fire on German planes; neighborhood playgrounds dug up and made into air raid shelters. There were also sandbag fortifications here and there, windows crisscrossed with tape to prevent flying glass during the bombing, and sixty-foot-long barrage balloons, raised to force enemy planes to fly

Geoffrey Shakespeare, head of the CORB program. His family tree includes William Shakespeare. [Wikimedia Commons]

around them. The hydrogen in the balloons would explode if hit, and their steel cables would send a plane crashing to the ground if it tried to fly under.

Then there were the bombs themselves. Some had hit right near the Keeley family's flat in south London, all along Brixton Road. One landed in the middle of the tram lines, one struck the gas main, and another hit a water main, which Jack thought was funny, the water spurting everywhere.

Jack did not think the bombs themselves were funny—he was glad to get away from them, especially the shrieking bombs, screeching louder and louder as they got closer to the ground. Those scared the life out of him.

British girls sit on a Nazi bomber that crashed near their house.
[Imperial War Museum]

THERE WERE OTHER children passengers not with CORB. Most of them were with their mothers. But Colin Ryder Richardson, eleven, was traveling alone, all the way to New York, to live with friends of his parents. Even if the United States entered the war on England's side—as it certainly would—his parents were sure Hitler would be stopped before he could invade the United States.

Colin's parents had moved the family out of London when the war started, and Colin and his little brother had been living on a farm in Wales for the past year. Colin loved his life on the farm, and he didn't want to leave. But his parents feared an invasion and had arranged for him to go to America. He bravely agreed, telling himself that it was a privilege. He'd sail with the others to Canada, and then travel to New York. His little brother, Julian, was staying home; his parents felt he was too young to go. And, although Colin didn't know this, his mother had been pregnant with a baby girl, who was stillborn in May 1938, just two years earlier. Colin's mother could not bear to send away both sons. It was painful enough to send one.

It wasn't an easy choice for any of the parents to make: Keep their children at home, a place that was now dangerous, or send them away for nobody knew how long? When war was first declared, many city parents had sent their children to villages in the countryside to be safer. That was a big step, but this, sending a child across the ocean, was more heart-wrenching.

In some families, like the Walders, children asked their parents to let them go. Some husbands and wives argued over the decision.

For one mother the choice was easy. Beth Cummings, fourteen, was very little when her father died, leaving her mother a widow. Beth's two older brothers were already serving in the war, so her mother had decided to *guarantee* the safety of one of her children.

Although she and her mother were very close, Beth was thrilled to be on this adventure. In the couple of days at the Liverpool school, Beth had become friends with Bess Walder. They had a lot in common: they had similar names; they were both from cities; they were both tall and sturdily built; and both were smart and determined. But Bess was quiet and reserved, while Beth was talkative, lively, and full of excitement, like Liverpool, her hometown. She told her new friend, We'll have a grand time at sea.

....

THE CHILDREN WEREN'T worried about the danger. The parents were. They knew they were taking a risk sending their children on a ship during wartime, that German U-boats were blowing up British ships. This is why they had to sign the disclaimer. But CORB officials assured the parents that their children would be safe.

The CORB program had already sent thousands of children to safety. Every ship that carried CORB children had Royal Navy warships—equipped with artillery—escorting and guarding it through dangerous waters.

Just a few weeks earlier, on August 30, the *Volendam*, another ship sailing from Liverpool and carrying a large CORB group, had been torpedoed by a German U-boat. The news service Reuters reported the incident with the *Volendam*: "A British evacuee ship on its way to Canada has been torpedoed by a U-boat in the Atlantic, but not a single child was lost. The vessel carried 320 children and other passengers, and the only casualty was a purser."

The article went on to say that the children had been trained in lifeboat drills, and when they were all safely in the lifeboats, they sang! They sang "Roll Out the Barrel" and "Oh, Johnny! Oh, Johnny, Oh!"

The article did not report that one child had slept through the whole incident. Crew members found him the next day on the damaged ship. He was fine, and reluctant to leave the ship since being the only child on board, he felt in charge. But it could have been worse. The part of the story of the boy left behind was kept quiet from the press—at Geoffrey Shakespeare's insistence.

The *Volendam* torpedo did scare some parents, and they pulled their children out of the CORB program. But most of the parents felt even more sure of their decision—because the worst had happened and the children had survived. Two children who had been on the *Volendam* were now in line to board the *Benares*. Their parents were confident that their children would be safe (though neither child would survive this journey).

All in all it seemed a good bet that the children would be safer at sea than at home, with the bombs raining down night after night. Even here in Liverpool, there had been bombs. The CORB group spent two nights in an underground shelter at the school, and a few children screamed in terror all night. The ship's departure was delayed because of the bombardment.

Now the children would be on their way to safety—and adventure.

Jack Keeley was looking forward to a better life. He was eager to get to Canada, which he thought of like America, where "everyone had swimming pools, everyone had cars, everyone was rich. No poor people in America or Canada, not to us."

And once they boarded the *City of Benares*, Jack and the other CORB children felt they were richer and luckier than they could ever have imagined.

CHAPTER 3

A Floating Palace

GUSSIE GRIMMOND WALKED up the steep gangplank with her sisters Violet and Connie. So did Eddie and Lennie Grimmond, Jack Keeley, Bess Walder, and Beth Cummings—all the CORB children. "We had our photo taken as we were coming on the boat," Gussie wrote to her parents later. (The photo did not survive.)

Jack Keeley was immediately bowled over by how large the ship was. Years later, he'd realize it wasn't as huge as it looked to a nine-year-old boy. But at this moment, it seemed titanic.

And so fancy. All the children were struck by the ship's grandeur.

The SS *City of Benares* was almost brand-new. The steam-powered ocean liner had been built in Glasgow, Scotland, just four years earlier, for the Ellerman City Line to carry passengers on the long voyage to India. The ship was designed, fitted, and furnished to feel luxurious, and from the time of its maiden voyage out of Liverpool in October 1936, the *Benares* was the largest and most modern ship in the Ellerman fleet.

LIBRARY

LOUNGE

BLE BEDSTEAD CABIN

DINING SALOON

VIEW FROM BRIDGE LOOKING AFT

PROMENADE DECK

SWIMMING BATH

England to India and back again was the ship's sole route in its first years, which is why it was named *City of Benares*, after the holy city on the Ganges now known as Varanasi. This trip to Canada was to be the liner's first transatlantic voyage, and its first trip for the CORB program.

The *Benares* had been brightly painted, but once Ellerman Lines offered it to the British government to use for the CORB program, the British Ministry of War had the ship repainted to attract less attention. The War Ministry also installed defensive artillery—large cannon-like guns to fire on attacking ships, U-boats, or planes—on its bow and stern. This was commonly done to merchant ships being used in wartime service.

Since the liner looked like a passenger ship but wasn't painted like one and had guns, the enemy wouldn't know what kind of ship it was or who it was carrying. There was no real way to indicate that children were on board. The ship couldn't fly a Red Cross flag because the *Benares* wasn't a hospital or Red Cross ship. It wasn't entirely on a humanitarian mission, either. Since so many of the passengers were part of a government program, the ship was offi-cially on war business. In discussing the scheme, one member of Parliament made the argument that the British government should announce that the ships were carrying children. "We should illumi-nate these ships and depend even on the Germans, not to do anything to the children on their journey across the ocean," he said. "I would be prepared to put that trust in humanity although it may be at a very low ebb." However, the Children's Overseas Reception Board decided against this.

In Parliament there was discussion on how best to sail to keep the CORB ships safe. There wasn't a perfect option. Should each CORB ship travel alone or in a convoy? German U-boats were attacking ships throughout the Atlantic. They had fired on ships traveling alone and in convoys. Government officials decided that a convoy would be safer. So the *Benares* was part of a convoy, with military escort ships.

Gussie, Bess, Jack, and the others weren't thinking of any of this. They were just excited.

. . . .

SO WAS FRED STEELS. He was eleven, originally from the fishing town of Hull in Yorkshire, on the east coast of England. Fred's parents had already suffered the loss of three children, and with the war on, they were scared for their son's life. They decided to keep him safe by sending him to Canada to live with relatives. The baby of the family, Audrey, was too young for the CORB program. She stayed home.

Fred seemed made for the sea. He had been born with a caul—a piece of membrane—over his face, which is considered a good luck charm against drowning. His mother sold it to the skipper of a fishing boat. Growing up, Fred knew many fishermen. He would go to the docks when the boats came in with the day's catch, and one of the fishermen usually gave him something to take home for his mum to cook for dinner. Here y'are, nippy, take this home to your mum, a fisherman would say, throwing Fred a huge cod that almost knocked him off his feet.

The small boats he had seen in Hull had not prepared him for *this* ship. Fred thought it was something out of this world, a floating palace. And as he boarded, he was hit with a strong smell of curry.

Indian spices did waft through the air on the *City of Benares*. The ship had forty-three crew members from Britain, but most of the crew was from India. The 166 lascars, as Indian sailors were called, served as deck crew, cooks, bakers, waiters, porters, kitchen helpers, pantry boys, cabin boys, and stewards. They worked in the engine room as fire stokers. There were two barbers, Muhammad Gulab and Muhammad Shafi. There were translators. Most, if not all, were Muslim. They came from very poor families and worked to support their relatives back home. We have the names of those who died, but only a few names of the many who survived. Because of the racism and classism of the time, we know little about the individuals who served. When all this was over, when the articles were written and the interviews conducted, the lascars were mostly ignored.

Many of the CORB children had never known a person with brown skin. Some of the children looked at the Indians with awe and excitement. Others with fear. Fear born of ignorance, which resulted, as for so many, in racism.

Gussie wrote home to her parents, "We have got plenty of dark men on this boat. They clean our shoes and clean our room for us. They do all the work when we are on deck. The dark men look at us, but we don't take any notice."

Bess, whose father brought home experience of a wider world, was thrilled to see, waiting for her and the other children, "Indian stewards wearing turbans and brilliant blue cummerbunds and shoes that turned up at the ends. We were in seventh heaven."

The lascars were dressed in lightweight clothes suitable for the ship's usual route to India. They were not dressed for the cold weather of the North Atlantic. Later the question would be asked, Why were they not given sailor uniforms or at least warmer clothing, appropriate to the climate they would be sailing through? On this journey their thin clothing would turn out to be impractical and in many cases deadly.

....

THE CORB ESCORTS took the children to their cabins and got them settled. "Eddie and Lennie are sharing a cabin," Gussie wrote to her parents. "Connie, Violet and me are sharing a cabin."

The new friends Bess Walder and Beth Cummings weren't put in the same cabin, but they were on the same hallway, right near each other. Beth had two roommates, a fifteen-year-old and a twelve-year-old, both also from Liverpool. Bess's roommates were ten-year-old Ailsa Murphy and twelve-year-old Patricia Allen, who had survived the *Volendam* torpedo. Patricia and ten-year-old Michael Brooker, the other *Volendam* child on the *Benares*, were homeless. Patricia's home had been badly damaged in a raid, and like the Grimmonds, her family was living in a homeless shelter. Michael's house had an unexploded bomb inside, and until it could be removed, his family was also in a shelter. Their parents thought it best to give CORB another try. Patricia and Michael were settling into ship cabins for the second time in just over two weeks.

The ninety CORB children were housed all together in the back end of the ship, on the lowest passenger deck. The forty-four girls slept on the port (left) side, the forty-six boys on the starboard. Usually the cabins had two regular beds, but for this journey they were furnished with bunk beds, making room for more children on board. Most of the cabins housed three children, though Bobby and John Baker, brothers from Southall, near London, were pleased to find they had a cabin to themselves. Not that little Johnny, seven, would spend much time in it—he had too much fun running around the ship.

The cabins had chests of drawers, night tables, and a clothing closet. "The cabins are all furnished," Gussie wrote home after they got settled. "Connie and Violet are sharing a wardrobe." There were railings on each side of the beds, at the head, so if the ship rocked in a storm, the sleeping passengers wouldn't fall out. But the furniture was not bolted down—which would turn out to be a serious danger. Each cabin had a porthole or a window, and a fan for circulation.

On an upper deck of the ship, eleven-year-old Colin Ryder Richardson met Laszlo Raskai, a young journalist from Hungary who worked for the BBC. Colin's parents had arranged for Laszlo to be Colin's chaperone. As it would turn out, they hardly saw each other. Colin went to bed before Laszlo got in for the night, and Laszlo was awake and out by the time Colin woke up. Colin didn't mind. Laszlo seemed nice enough, but Colin could take care of himself; he did not need a guardian. In a few nights, though, Laszlo would take his role as guardian very seriously, and Colin would be grateful.

Now Colin unpacked. He took out his comic books and his clothes. Most important was the life jacket his mother had given him. She'd had it custom-made, and it didn't look like a regular life vest: it had long sleeves, pockets, and a collar. It buttoned up like an ordinary jacket and was made of bright red silk. All the children had life preservers, of course, padded kapok vests in addition to the canvas-covered cork ones all the passengers were given. But Colin's mother was sure this special jacket would work much better than anything the ship would give him—and it would be more comfortable, too. Comfort was important, because she made Colin promise to wear it all the time, day and night. She assured her son that if the ship got torpedoed and sank, the Royal Navy would rescue them. But he had to wear his jacket so he'd be certain to survive.

Colin put on his red jacket and wore it all day from the very first. Everyone on the upper decks got to know him right away because of it. The color prompted someone to nickname him Will Scarlet, after one of Robin Hood's Merry Men.

....

NOT FAR FROM COLIN, there was a mother and three children. Sonia Bech, also eleven, got unpacked in her cabin, which she shared with her big sister, Barbara, fourteen. Barbara tried to open their porthole, but she soon realized it was painted shut. On the upper decks, above the waterline, the portholes were blacked out so no lights could shine through, a wartime precaution just like back home. The war had followed them onto the ship.

Their nine-year-old brother, Derek, was in a cabin two doors away with their mother.

With the threat of war, Mrs. Bech had moved Sonia, Barbara, and Derek out of London to their summer house in a gated neighborhood on the southern coast of England.

The children loved their summer house. They played in the sand and had picnics with their Danish nanny, Meta. Every summer afternoon the ice cream man came to the beach on his tricycle. The adults had fun, too—big parties with dancing, and midnight swimming.

Living there full-time, Sonia and Barbara and Derek rode their bikes all over the neighborhood with complete freedom. Their favorite game was called prison. Some children were the police, and some were criminals, and the police chased the criminals all over on their bikes. When caught, the "villains" were locked up in the shed behind the Bechs' house. Sonia and Barbara and Derek did not miss living in London at all.

But when the war came to England, it came to the coast where the Bechs lived. The Tangmere airfield, a Royal Air Force fighter station, was right nearby. Derek and his friend used to watch the planes take off and land. When the Germans started bombing the airfields, there were dogfights in the sky right above them, even during the day. And planes sometimes crashed nearby. When Derek saw a plane go down, he would hop on his bike and pedal as fast as he could to the scene. He was often the first one there and had a good view of the planes.

He witnessed so many crashes that he could tell the smell of British oil from German oil. Afterward, he'd gather pieces from the downed airplanes. He had quite a collection of bits of German aircraft and shrapnel and even machine gun bullets. He took his treasures to school in a suitcase.

What have you got today? his classmates would ask. To Derek it was a big treasure hunt.

One day he brought an actual bomb back home, to the dismay of his mother.

Where on earth did you get that? Mrs. Bech demanded.

Derek didn't think it was such a big deal. It was "just" an incendiary, not a big bomb.

But his mother had it put in the back "prison" shed and called the police to remove it. Derek was sorry to see the bomb go, but at least he had the rest of his collection.

The war wasn't all fun and games, though. Derek also had a close-up view of death. One day he and his friend saw the burned bodies of English and German pilots who had crashed. Another day, he heard planes and looked up in time to see a terrible accident: two British Spitfires cut each other in half, crashing to the ground. Derek raced to the scene on his bike, but fortunately this time someone else got there first and blocked his view: one of the pilots had been decapitated as he tried to bail out.

So their mother decided to take the children to Canada to live with relatives. Their father would stay in London, running his business.

Derek was sorry to leave his home and especially his tabby cat, Tim. But this trip was part of the adventure of the war. And even though he couldn't bring Tim, Derek could bring his favorite toys.

Unlike the CORB kids, the paying passengers could bring whatever they wanted. Derek unpacked a big fire truck with a detachable hose, and an ambulance with a stretcher inside. He also had his suitcase full of war souvenirs; he couldn't leave that behind.

Sonia didn't want to leave, either. She would miss her nanny, the beach, and especially her Scottie dog, Mackie. She'd been allowed to bring her favorite doll, John, though. John had gone to the hospital with her a few weeks earlier, when she had to have her tonsils and adenoids out. He was outfitted with pajamas and a bathrobe exactly like hers. He even had a little suitcase. And now he was going to Canada with her.

At fourteen Barbara was embarrassed to be leaving. That summer the whole country   the Bechs included—had heard Winston Churchill's rallying cry after British forces were evacuated from Dunkirk when the Nazis invaded France: "We shall fight on the beaches, we shall fight on the landing grounds, we shall fight in the fields and in the streets, we shall fight in the hills; we shall never surrender."

To make Barbara feel even worse, her cousin, a Royal Air Force pilot, had accused her family of being rats leaving a sinking ship.

Barbara could see that going to Canada made sense for her younger brother and sister, as well as her mother, but not for her. It seemed like desertion. In fact, Churchill had not been in favor of the CORB program, for just this reason. But the prime minister had let it go through—some thought because he was too distracted and upset by the fall of France to Hitler, which occurred during the time the CORB decision was being made.

In any case, Barbara had no choice—her mother would not leave her behind.

In the cabin with Derek, their mother, Marguerite, put her special travel bag in a safe place. It contained what she considered her most valuable items: money, passports, other important papers, and a small round metal jewelry box. Inside the box, which was lined with green felt, were four rings and a diamond brooch. Mrs. Bech also put a flask of brandy in her travel bag. You never knew what might happen, and the brandy would make her feel warm on a cold night at sea. (Alcohol actually lowers the body temperature, so drinking it when you are cold is not a good idea and can be dangerous. People did not know this back then.)

....

ALL OVER THE SHIP, passengers were settling in, and the children were exploring. Everyone was looking forward to setting sail.

But the ship would not set sail for Canada that day. It would just sail a little bit away from the docks and the city. German bombers had dropped mines at the mouth of the river Mersey, and the area had to be cleared before ships could head out to sea. The *Benares* would have to wait out the traffic jam in the river.

Before the war, every day at one in the afternoon, a cannon was fired from Birkenhead, across the river from the Liverpool docks, so ships could check to make sure their chronometers were accurate. With the war on, the one o'clock cannon did not fire, but that was when—on September 12—the SS *City of Benares* pulled away.

It sailed past the Victoria Clock Tower, with its six-sided "docker's clock," and farther out into the river, toward the bay, and anchored there. The *City of Benares* would stay near Liverpool at least one more night.

....

GUSSIE GRIMMOND STARTED writing to her parents before they left the docks. She wanted them to receive a letter as soon as possible. She would make her sisters write, too. There was already so much to say. The Grimmond girls' letters would be mailed before the ship pulled anchor.

Gussie couldn't know that their letters would arrive a week later, along with another letter, this one bringing official—and terrible—news to the Grimmond parents.

Victoria Clock Tower at Liverpool Docks [Wikimedia Commons]

CHAPTER 4

Desserts and Drills

IT IS VERY lovely," Gussie wrote. "I wish you were with us." She told her parents that she and her siblings were going to have their photos taken for a second time. They were drinking milk.

She assured her mother that the CORB people had taken care of them since they had not been able to pack anything: "Please, mum, do not worry as we have been fitted up with clothes."

Gussie was pleased with the clothes. Back at the Liverpool school, she had told Bess Walder, Oh, if my mum could see me now!

But what excited Gussie the most was the dining room. All the CORB children were thrilled with the food. One boy later reminisced that it seemed such a long way to go up to the dining room on the next deck—three flights of stairs—but it was worth it!

The tables in the dining room were set with china plates, cloth napkins, and silverware. Many of the children hadn't ever been to a restaurant, hadn't ever seen a table set this way.

The cooks and waiters were used to preparing and serving fancy dinners on this ship. Notes to the staff on an earlier cruise included instructions such as, "No bread on table. Bread to be handed round in baskets . . . Napkins laid flat on table and turned over." Also, "in serving asparagus, lay fork right hand side and tilt hot plate on fork." The menu on that cruise had included caviar, lobster, kidneys (to be cooked "underdone"), potatoes scraped and boiled with plenty of fresh mint in the water, chicken curry, and duckling stewed in brown gravy, served with cherry sauce.

Some of the children came from families with little money, and so even without wartime rationing they didn't have a big variety of food or a lot of it—no dessert, and chicken only on Christmas. Now they could have both, and as much as they wanted.

Gussie wrote home, "We go into a big room for meals and we have silver knives and fork, we have table napkins and three different kinds of forks." And, "We have a menu card in which we can choose what we like off the card. There are about a dozen different things on it."

With war rationing, food back home was limited. Bess Walder's family wasn't poor, and they had plenty of food, but this was something else! She hadn't seen a banana for years, and here they were on the ship, for the taking. All she had to do was clap her hands, and one of the waiters would come right over with whatever she wanted.

May I have a ham roll? she'd ask.

And very quickly the waiter would come back with not one but two ham rolls. And they were presented on a silver tray lined with a lace cloth.

Even for the Bechs, the dining experience was out of the ordinary. Sonia was charmed by the Indian waiters in their lovely clothes, willing to give her as much food as she wanted. The waiters spoiled the children like mad, and the children loved it.

For Jack Keeley, this was a totally different world from what he was used to—all the food and the men waiting on him. He was being treated like a prince. And the ice cream—so much of it, so many different flavors. He couldn't believe that he could have as many helpings of ice cream as he wanted. And he did! He had two, sometimes three!

They all loved the ice cream.

Those who survived would remember, even decades later, that the loss of all that ice cream felt like a terrible tragedy.

....

AS IF THE FOOD weren't great enough, the children had a playroom. Violet Grimmond, ten, wrote to her parents, "We have a play room to play in." The walls had characters from fairy tales and myths painted on them.

Gussie wrote, "The little ones have got a nursery to play in and a big store sent them a box of toys. Lennie goes about as if nothing is happening."

Unlike Derek Bech, the CORB kids weren't able to bring toys, and some of them—like the Grimmonds—had none to bring anyway.

There was a Noah's ark with little wooden animals in pairs, pull toys, stuffed animals, toy soldiers, and a grand rocking horse, with a basket on either side so three children could ride it. The rocking horse quickly became the talk of the group—even the older kids, who weren't allowed into the room to play, heard about the magnificent rocking horse.

A few nights later, when the younger children were asleep, Bess Walder would sneak into the playroom so she could ride the famous horse herself. She rocked just a little, and then rushed out.

UPSTAIRS ON THE PROMENADE DECK, Colin Ryder Richardson, in his scarlet-red life jacket, found the library. It was a beautiful room paneled in Nigerian cherry, mahogany, and holly. Both Colin and Barbara Bech would spend a lot of time in here reading.

The library curved under the forward end of the bridge deck, and normally passengers could look out to the sea on both the port and starboard sides. But for this voyage all the library's windows were blacked out so that no lights could shine at night. Also on the promenade deck was a lounge for paying passengers, with carpeting, comfortable upholstered chairs, tables, a dance floor, a cocktail bar, and a card room.

The lounge was the muster station for Colin and the Bech family. All passengers were assigned a muster station—where they would gather in the event of an attack or an accident. Everyone was assigned a lifeboat station, too, where they would go from their muster station during drills—or a real emergency. The ship had twelve lifeboats, with enough room for 494 people, more than were on board. There were also twenty-two life rafts, enough for 292 people.

. . . .

EACH OF THE CORB ESCORTS was given a sheet explaining the rules of the ship, the lifeboat drills, and what to do in case of an emergency:

EMERGENCY ARRANGEMENTS
SS "CITY OF BENARES"

NOTES ON EMERGENCY DRILL AND "ABANDON SHIP"
FOR THE GUIDANCE OF ESCORTS

1. Alarm-Signal. Continuous ringing alarm gongs.

2. The Signal in case of emergency is seven
   short blasts and one long blast on the ship's
   whistle, supplemented by the ringing of the
   Electric alarm gongs. (The steam whistle is
   also used in the navigation of the ship when
   manoeuvring, altering course, and in fog, but
   the longest signal normally used at sea on
   these occasions is three blasts only, so there
   should be no possibility of confusion.)

3. Your duty on hearing the Alarm Signal is to see
   that the children under your care get their
   Lifebelts and suitable clothes, and proceed to
   the Assembly Station allotted for your group.
   Do not forget your own Lifebelt. The KAPOK
   Lifebelts provided are suitable for children,
   and care must be taken that the tapes are
   tied as tightly as possible: this should be
   impressed on all children capable of tying
   their own Lifebelts.

4. You should familiarize yourself with your
   Assembly Station and notices with DIRECTION
   ARROWS are placed in the alleyways to indicate
   the route. The Stewards will give you all
   assistance and guidance in this matter.
   To each group of children have been allotted
   certain of the ship's crew whose only duty in

an emergency is to help the escort. Get to know who is attached to your group as soon as possible.

5. A Boat Muster Drill will be held on board daily, and the ship's Medical Officers will be in attendance for Medical inspection of the children.

THE FOLLOWING RULES WHILE ON BOARD ARE BROUGHT TO YOUR ATTENTION.

(1) Children must not put their heads out of the port holes or attempt to open or close ports or dead-lights.

(2) Children must not climb on the ship's rails.

(3) Without instructions from their escort or the ship's officials, children must not leave the accommodation allotted to them.

(4) Children will not be allowed on the upper decks during the hours of darkness, or when coming alongside or leaving any landing stages, or at any other time when the winches are being worked or ropes handled on their parts of the upper deck.

(5) Passengers are strictly prohibited from striking matches, exhibiting lights or smoking on deck after dark.

LIVERPOOL

SEPTEMBER, 1940

THE FIRST LIFEBOAT DRILL occurred after the ship had moved away from the docks into the river, about three o'clock in the afternoon.

Connie Grimmond wrote home, "Me, Gussie and Violet feed the seagulls . . . When we was having milk the bells went for every baby to go and put on lifebelts."

When the alarm sounded, everyone went to the muster stations, and then to the lifeboats. In case of emergency, the children would get into the lifeboats and then the boats would be lowered down the side of the ship to the sea. The lifeboats were lowered using small cranes called davits. The crew did not practice the lowering during the drills.

Colin and the Bechs went to the lounge, where they met each other for the first time. Colin and Sonia were the same age, and they all became friends right away. Sonia got an immediate crush on Colin. He had blond hair, light blue eyes, and a sweet, wide smile. She thought he was gorgeous.

There were ten children and teens among the paying passengers; Colin and the Bechs were four of them. Since CORB children were segregated in their parts of the ship, and ate at different times from the paying passengers, Colin and the Bechs had no idea that ninety other children were aboard, many of them just their age, also having lifeboat drills.

The CORB children went with their chaperones to their muster stations. Gussie and her sisters went with Mary Cornish, and Gussie reported to her parents that the drills were "in case our boat got hit." She also told them about their chaperone. "Our escort is a very nice lady, Miss Cornish," Gussie wrote, "but we call her Auntie Mary."

Mary was impressed by Gussie from the very start, especially how she made sure her sisters—and her brothers when she could— behaved correctly. Gussie was particularly attentive in the dining room, where she made her siblings sit still and use the proper silverware.

Gussie put her sisters' letters with hers and got them ready to mail, but not before she told her parents, "Our boat is in the middle of the river. We are all eager to start off. While we were on the boat last night there were two air raid warnings, but we were asleep."

And she reassured them: "There are men to guard us at night in case our boat got sunk."

She asked her parents to forgive her writing and spelling and sent love from her and sisters and brothers. And she wrote, "Please do not answer this letter for I will be in mid-Atlantic."

These lascars served on another ocean liner used for war service. The Viceroy *was also torpedoed by a German U-boat. All but four of the crew survived, as did all of the passengers. The crew on the* City of Benares *dressed similarly.* [Marine Photo Service, National Maritime Museum]

CHAPTER 5

Wish Me Luck as You Wave Me Goodbye

THE *CITY OF BENARES* would be the lead ship in a convoy of nineteen vessels. In addition to the *Benares*, Convoy OB-213 included oil tankers, steamships, freighters, and smaller commercial boats. They would have three Royal Navy escorts: a destroyer called HMS *Winchelsea* and two smaller warships, the Flower class corvettes *Gladiolus* and *Gloxinia.*

The escort vessels' job was to keep the convoy safe and warn the other vessels, especially the *Benares*, if U-boats were in the area. The destroyer would travel three miles ahead, zigzagging independently to listen for U-boats with its special radar. Should a U-boat attack—which was unlikely with the Royal Navy destroyer present—the *Winchelsea* would save passengers and drop depth charges (bombs that explode underwater) onto the enemy submarine.

Landles Nicoll was captain of the *City of Benares*. But also traveling on his ship was Admiral Edmond Mackinnon, commodore of the whole convoy. Captain Nicoll was in command of his ship, but Admiral Mackinnon could overrule Nicoll. That would become a crucial issue in a few days. Now, however, the two men agreed: the ship would sail the next day, Friday, September 13.

When Mrs. Bech heard the date the ship was going to sail, she didn't like it at all. Some consider thirteen an unlucky number, and Friday the thirteenth an unlucky day. It wasn't the first thirteen that had cropped up: Derek Bech had noticed that when they left Euston Station for Liverpool, they had left from platform thirteen.

In addition to the Friday-the-thirteenth superstition, in sailing lore it is considered bad luck to embark on a journey on *any* Friday. So the sailors would have been much happier to wait until Saturday the fourteenth. But the captain and the commodore had more than superstition to consider. They had to factor in the schedule of the Royal Navy escorts assigned to protect the convoy and the CORB children. The naval ships had to turn around in five days and escort a convoy coming in from Canada with food, gas, and other supplies for England. If the *Benares* was to have protection through all the perilous waters, as the CORB parents had been promised, it would have to sail on Friday the thirteenth.

....

WHEN THE *BENARES* lifted anchor and began to pull out of the river Mersey, it had 215 crew members, 91 paying passengers, and the CORB group of 10 volunteer escorts and 90 children, for a total of 406 people aboard. Marguerite Bech had kept her family on board, even though the date scared her.

Jack Keeley and Bess Walder and Beth Cummings and Fred Steels, along with Gussie, Violet, Connie, Eddie, and Lennie Grimmond and the other CORB children (except the homesick ones), shouted and waved and cheered. It was the custom of the CORB children to sing as the ship began the journey. Their favorite songs were "There'll Always Be an England":

> May this fair land we love so well
> in dignity and freedom dwell.
> Tho' worlds may change and go awry
> while there's still one voice to cry—
> There'll always be an England. . . .
> Freedom remains. These are the chains
> nothing can break.

And "My Bonnie Lies over the Ocean":

> My Bonnie lies over the ocean,
> My Bonnie lies over the sea,
> My Bonnie lies over the ocean,
> Oh bring back my Bonnie to me!

And "Wish Me Luck (as You Wave Me Goodbye)":

> Cheerio, here I go, on my way.
> Wish me luck as you wave me goodbye
> with a cheer, not a tear, make it gay.
> Give me a smile I can keep all the while
> in my heart while I'm away.

....

WHEN THE CORB CHIEF spoke to children before their journey, he reminded them that they were "little ambassadors" for England. They represented their great country both on the journey and once they landed in their new homes.

In setting up the program, government officials had another motive: if most of the children who stayed in England died during the war, those who had spent the war in faraway countries could repopulate the land once England and its allies were victorious.

"There'll always be an England," the song ended, "and England shall be free, if England means as much to you as England means to me."

....

BUT NOW, AS THE SHIP SAILED into the Irish Sea toward the Atlantic Ocean, the children weren't thinking about being ambassadors or about the future of England or anything serious like that. They were all thinking of their next meal and of the fun they would have on this grand ship.

All but a few, that is: some, like little Joyce Keeley, still cried; they wanted to go back home to their mothers.

....

THE *CITY OF BENARES* left Liverpool behind, sailing past Fort Perch Rock and the lighthouse, whose beam could be seen for miles. There had been a gale reported in the Irish Sea, and when the ship reached open water, the winds blew strong and the waves got high—and higher. The ship rolled and rocked, making many of the passengers, including some of the children, terribly seasick.

The German war submarine U-boat 48 had been at sea for five days, navigating the rolling sea through stormy weather. On the same day that the *Benares* set sail, the U-boat commander ordered a dive. He wanted to give his crew a break from the bad weather. The radio engineer entered this into his log that night, per usual. And the U-boat crew had a warm meal and relief from the storm in the calm waters beneath the surface.

On the *Benares*, the children who weren't seasick, who got their "sea legs" quickly, ran about the rolling ship, exploring. And soon the seas calmed down, and most of the children became used to the gentler rocking. Marjorie Day, the head escort, established a routine for the CORB children.

There were regular school lessons—though these were not mandatory. The escorts also taught the children about Canada so that they might know more about the land where they were going to live. And some of the escorts led special activities scheduled around everyone's favorite thing—the meals.

Mary Cornish, whom *all* the children now loved and called Auntie Mary, formed a chorus. Most of the girls enjoyed the chorus; most of the boys did not. Sybil Gilliat-Smith, twenty-five, was an artist and art teacher. She gave drawing lessons to the children and held a drawing contest, which was very popular.

Michael Rennie, twenty-three, was the youngest of the CORB

Above: *A type VIIB U-boat* [Wikimedia Commons] · Opposite: *Michael Rennie's application to become a CORB escort.*
[The National Archives (Britain)/CORB]

APPLICATION F.

Children's Overseas Reception Board,
Thomas Cook's Buildings,
10, Mayfair Place,
London, W.1.

I desire to offer my services under the scheme for accompanying children overseas.

Full name (in block capitals) **MICHAEL RENNIE** (Single)

No. on Identity Card **BKEE / 85 / 3.**

Nationality **BRITISH (C. of E.)**   *Due to take "Holy Orders"*
just down from Keble College, Ox.

Date of Birth **5/8/17 (23)**
? military age – exempt.

Address **S. JUDE'S VICARAGE, HAMPSTEAD GARDEN SUBURB**
N.W

What experience have you had –

(a) in controlling and looking after groups of children.
Monitor at Christ's Hospital both in the Senior school and had charge of number of Preparatory boys

(b) in the welfare of children
A Boy Scout for 17 years.

(c) in sea travelling North sea crossings + sailing.

Names and addresses of two references The WARDEN, KEBLE, COLLEGE, OXFORD
BISHOP CROTTY, 31, GORDON SQUARE, W.C.

I shall be available for the following period (or periods) FROM NOW UNTIL 10ᵗʰ OCTOBER.

Signature Michael Rennie

Date 8 JULY 1940.

Please send to address shown at top.

escorts, and the favorite among the boys. He organized games of tennis and tug-of-war, and he taught his group how to lasso deck chairs. He even organized a lassoing contest with the chairs. Louis Walder, Bess's brother, was in Michael's group and admired him greatly. Michael, the son of a vicar, was smart, handsome, and athletic. He played rugby and tennis, sailed, and was a scout. He also was a genius at mechanical things, especially with cars, which he loved. His favorite thing was to fix up old cars and race them against expensive new ones. When he was in high school, he kept an old junker behind his house. Michael had planned to be an engineer, and he already had interest from a car maker in something he had invented and patented—a device that made a car unusable to anyone but its owner. But when someone he admired, a priest and housing reformer named Basil Jellicoe, died, Michael heard a calling to the church. So after this voyage, when he returned home to north London, he would be off to divinity school. But now he concentrated on entertaining the CORB boys. Luckily for them, he was great with younger children. He had been a monitor at his boarding school, and the younger boys there had loved him for his laugh and his understanding. One of those students wrote in a tribute later that he had modeled himself after Michael Rennie.

Michael, Mary, Sybil, and the other escorts also became bankers. Most of the children had a little pocket money from their parents, to spend both on the ship and once they arrived in Canada. But it was difficult not to spend it all at once, so it was soon decided that the adults better handle it.

The children gave their money to their escort, who wrote down in a book exactly how much each child had. If a child wanted to buy a bar of chocolate—Louis Walder adored chocolate; his favorite was Cadbury Dairy Milk—or some boiled sweets (hard candy) or an ice pop from the ship's canteen, the child would run to the escort and ask for the amount needed. The escort would dole out the child's money and mark down how much was taken. At the end of the trip all the unspent money would be given back to the child to use in Canada. Some children already had plans for spending it there, especially on their birthdays. They wanted big, creamy birthday cakes, and one boy knew that there would be a pony he could ride near his new home in Canada, so his pocket money was going to that!

Later, after disaster struck, this pocket money would become a huge concern for six of the boys.

....

THERE WAS EVEN MORE EXCITEMENT: the children would be in a movie. A glamorous woman named Ruby Grierson had been hanging around with them on board. Ruby was making a documentary film about the CORB children for the Canadian government. Many of the children were eager to be near her—and not only to get in the film. She looked like a movie star herself, with her movie camera, a cigarette dangling from her lips, and a beret on her head. And she walked around the ship wearing trousers, not a dress or skirt, very unusual for a woman in 1940. Ruby filmed the children as they ate, played, sang, and sat for lessons.

One of the other passengers on the ship, Arthur Wimperis, worked in the movies, too. He was a screenwriter on his way to Hollywood to help write a script for a movie based on the popular novel *Mrs. Miniver*, about the life of a British woman just before the war. In the movie, the war would play a big part, and "a young girl at the height of her loveliness" would die. Now, on the ship, Wimperis watched the CORB children run around, sit for lessons, and play.

Most of the CORB boys didn't sit still for long. When they weren't in structured activities—or even if they were meant to be—they ran around the ship. They weren't really supposed to, but the crew didn't mind. The boys loved to watch the sailors at their various tasks, cleaning and checking equipment, arranging supplies, sifting lentils, washing rice.

The sailors were as strong and admirable as any movie hero or the ranchers the boys hoped to see in Canada. The sailors coiled and uncoiled the lines—ropes as thick as fire hoses, heavy as metal—as if they were mere jump ropes. The boys watched and asked questions. Jack Keeley was one who asked a lot of questions.

The boys also loved to look over the rails at the other boats in the convoy and wave. Sometimes the sailors on other boats waved back.

Johnny Baker got a reputation as the boy who kept getting lost. He ran around the ship so fast that his twelve-year-old brother, Bobby, couldn't stay with him—or maybe he just gave up. Bobby and Johnny came from Southall, a suburb west of London. There were ten people from Southall on the ship: the Baker boys, seven other CORB children, and one adult. Only one of those people would see Southall again.

Southall was feeling more and more dangerous, and Bobby and Johnny's parents wanted to get them away from the bombs. The boys were going to live in Vancouver, on the west coast of Canada. Their mother had two sisters there, and they were going to live with one of them. Vancouver would be a big change for the Baker boys. And the ship sure was. Such luxury. At home, their mother washed clothing by hand, with a coal fire and a washboard in the scullery in the kitchen corner. She used a mangle to wring water from the wet laundry.

Their dad delivered milk by a horse-drawn cart. He also worked as a joiner, constructing wooden parts for buildings—doors and door frames, stairs, window frames. Mr. Baker had fought in the First World War and had a scar on his wrist from when he was shot running away from the enemy. He would show Bobby and Johnny his scar and say, This is from running away. But he never complained about his wound; it didn't bother him when he sawed and hammered—only when someone grabbed his wrist right on the scar.

He was a tall man, from a family of tall men, and nothing got him too angry or upset. When Johnny misbehaved, his father never hit him, Johnny remembered later. He'd just pick him up by the collar and tell him quietly "what was what." That was enough to calm Johnny.

But unlike their dad, Bobby had no control over Johnny. Like all the older siblings, Bobby had been told to watch over his little brother. But he just couldn't keep following him all over the ship. Johnny was so fast—running here and there, going down gangways, around corners, up or down stairs. And then he would get lost. He'd stop, look around, and have no idea where he was. He'd try one way and then another, ask whomever he saw, Which way to the children's quarters? Eventually he would find his way back to Bobby.

When disaster struck, Bobby would not let Johnny run away. He would take care of his brother. But disaster was still a couple of days away. For now, there was fun.

. . . .

IN THE UPPER PART OF THE SHIP, Colin Ryder Richardson and the Bechs were enjoying themselves.

To the adults, "Will Scarlet" seemed very mature—walking around by himself in his bright red silk life jacket. He'd often be in the ship's library reading, or looking around to see how the ship worked. Sometimes Colin would wander into the bar, and the ladies would give him the maraschino cherries from their cocktails.

Because of Laszlo Raskai's schedule, Colin had all the freedom he wanted. Sometimes the Bech children would come over to his cabin for hours to play ghosts and other games.

And just like Michael Rennie, Colin invented a game with deck chairs, and got Barbara, Sonia, and Derek Bech to play with him. When it was windy, which it was often, they assembled the chairs and put them on the upwind side of the ship; the wind would send the chairs whooshing across the deck to the other side. Derek Bech watched in wonder as his new friend made the deck chairs float like sailing ships. They were having a whale of a time!

Close friendships were formed very quickly. Down in their part of the ship, Bess Walder and Beth Cummings cemented theirs. When they weren't helping to take care of the younger girls, they snuck away to a special nook they'd found near the children's playroom. There they could talk without being disturbed, and they'd tell each other stories about their lives before the trip.

Back at home, Bess had gotten into a little trouble with her parents. She was a serious girl, and determined, so when she saw that because of the war young women were working, she decided she would quit school and try to get a job. One morning, instead of going to school, she went to the local labor exchange. She asked for a job, not realizing that she'd given herself away as too young to work by wearing her school uniform, complete with blazer, Panama hat, and book bag. The people at the office saw the uniform, called the school, and found her parents. Her father came and got her.

Bess was mostly an obedient girl, and responsible, and that's why she was feeling guilty about her brother. Actually, she was having very mixed feelings about Louis. She was not watching out for him, as her father had asked. She did see him at mealtimes, and he seemed to be doing just fine, but she felt selfish because it was actually a relief not to have to supervise him, rambunctious boy that he was. Before too long, this guilt would come to haunt her—and maybe even save her life.

In contrast, Beth didn't have mixed feelings about anything. She knew she was in the right place. She would be safe, and her mother wouldn't have to worry about her. Beth was carefree and happy. So far, nothing had held her back from simply enjoying the trip.

CHAPTER 6

·····················

Secrets at Sea

BACK HOME IN BRITAIN, Sunday, September 15, was the heaviest tally of bombing yet. But the Royal Air Force pilots fought back and shot down more planes than ever before. People all over the country cheered as the number was announced: they'd gotten 185 German planes in one day.

Although the Brits didn't know it yet, Hitler had been rethinking his land invasion, Operation Sea Lion. Witnessing the British fortitude and determination to fight back, Hitler told his generals he would not attempt an invasion if it proved too dangerous. On September 17, Hitler would postpone the plan indefinitely.

On the *City of Benares*, they didn't have this news, and anyway, the war seemed far away, especially to the children. Life was grand: playing games, buying treats with pocket money, following around the glamorous Ruby Grierson with her movie camera, watching the ship's crew . . . and then there were the meals. The meals remained the most exciting part of the day; no one got tired of all the choices and the many flavors of ice cream.

Unfortunately, a couple of the littler boys, Alan Capel and Peter Short, both five years old, came down with chicken pox. They were put in the infirmary. Their older brothers, Derek Capel and Bill Short, were not sick.

One of the CORB escorts, Father Rory O'Sullivan, was terribly sick, not with chicken pox but with the flu, or perhaps extreme seasickness. He was so miserable that he couldn't lead Catholic Mass on Sunday as he had intended. But there were other church services, and other escorts pitched in and helped watch his boys.

The next day, the news of England's success in the air battle reached the ship. Everyone was thrilled! It seemed that their brave air force was holding the Germans at bay and that the war in England would be over soon.

That evening at dinner they had a party, which Ruby Grierson filmed. The CORB children wore party hats and made a racket with noisemakers.

But the celebration was premature.

As Captain Nicoll knew, the *Benares* and her passengers were not in the clear. They were still in dangerous waters. The crew had spotted a German bomber, and the telegraph operator had received reports of at least one U-boat in the area. Admiral Mackinnon ordered the convoy to coordinate zigzag maneuvers to confuse the U-boats.

After a few hours, no more U-boat warnings came. But Captain Nicoll was still worried about the danger. He wanted to get his ship far away from likely action quickly. The *Benares* could sail faster than any of the others in the convoy, and he would have liked to do that now. In fact, he would have liked to have been on his own for the whole journey, with sole control of his ship's movements, as he told his eldest daughter before he left home. He wasn't confident that the naval escort would guarantee that his ship—and the children on board—would make it to Canada safely.

Captain Nicoll, fifty-one, was a professional seaman. He was squarely built, strong, and steady. He was friendly but independent.

He was devoted to his family—his wife and three daughters—and wanted to get home to them. He also wanted very much to protect the children on the ship. They were his responsibility, one that he took seriously.

While having dinner at the captain's table, one of the guests asked Captain Nicoll if he would have sent his own daughters away. I'd as soon put their hands in the fire, he replied.

Now Captain Nicoll wanted to break away from the convoy as soon as possible. Although he was resigned to sailing with the Royal Navy escort, he planned to leave the convoy once the naval ships left. But as he talked about his intentions with Admiral Mackinnon, it became clear that the commodore did not agree. Mackinnon wanted to keep the convoy together.

Nicoll did not like that idea at all.

On the bridge—the ship's control room—Captain Nicoll and Admiral Mackinnon discussed their options. Admiral Mackinnon was sixty years old and had served with distinction in the First World War. He had retired in 1933, seven years earlier, but was recalled to help out in this war. He was older than Nicoll and used to being in charge. Reportedly, the tension between them grew. They argued.

The commanders may have had one more thing to consider— other precious cargo on this ship, not just the children. The *Benares* is likely to have been carrying gold, whose worth today would be more than twelve billion dollars. Ships carried gold as payment to the United States and Canada for weapons and other supplies to aid in the war effort against Germany.

The Germans would have been aware that some British ships carried this precious cargo, which was another reason to attack as many as possible. If you destroy a ship carrying gold, you not only whittle down the enemy's fleet but also diminish its resources.

Also on the ship were two politicians, an outspoken anti-Hitler German and a British politician who was going to America to raise funds for a volunteer ambulance corps. If the Germans knew they were on board, that would make the ship an even more valuable target. In any case, with the U-boat war so strong in the North Atlantic, both Nicoll and Mackinnon had to know it was likely the Germans would be after a ship this size.

....

IN THE VERY EARLY HOURS of September 17, 1940, HMS *Winchelsea*, HMS *Gloxinia*, and HMS *Gladiolus* left the convoy, as had been planned.

Now was decision time. The Royal Navy escort was gone. The *Benares* captain and the convoy commodore discussed their options. Captain Nicoll knew that Admiral Mackinnon would have the final say, but the captain was certain that dispersing the convoy was the best plan despite Mackinnon's desire to keep the ships together. Nicoll argued his point. Alone, the *Benares* could sail much faster and move farther away from the U-boats and danger.

A storm had started up, and that probably went into Mackinnon's reasoning. A torpedo attack was less likely in stormy weather. In high seas, it was more difficult to see the ships and harder for U-boats to aim torpedoes correctly and hit their targets. U-boats rarely tried to take down a ship in a storm.

Even eleven-year-old Colin Ryder Richardson knew that bad weather meant safety. Wandering around the ship, he had picked up a small ball bearing somewhere. He put it in the drawer next to his bed. As he lay there at night, he was reassured whenever he heard it rolling back and forth. That meant the water was choppy, and he was safe.

Mackinnon made his decision. He ordered the convoy to stay together.

The storm worsened. Captain Nicoll ordered passengers to stay belowdecks.

....

ON THIS VERY SAME DAY, Adolf Hitler called off his plan to invade Britain's homeland. He knew, however, that his navy could still hurt the country by sea.

Lurking in the North Atlantic near Mackinnon's convoy was a German U-boat, U-48. The captain of the U-boat and his crew had been watching the outbound convoy since about ten o'clock that morning. They had circled in front and in back. They were baffled— and happy—to see no Royal Navy escort. If the storm didn't get in his way, the commander had a plan. He would attack the lead ship first, then the others. He had the lead ship in his sights, although he didn't know its name: the SS *City of Benares*.

CHAPTER 7

U-boat 48

THE COMMANDER OF the U-boat, Kapitänleutnant Heinrich Bleichrodt, was not quite thirty-one years old; his birthday was in a month. Ajax, as he was called—a nickname he'd had since childhood—had started out as a sailor in the merchant marine and had been in the Kriegsmarine, the German navy, since before the war began. He'd been on U-boats for several years, but this was his first stint as a commander. He'd taken charge only two weeks earlier.

His submarine, U-48, was a type VIIB, more powerful and agile than earlier models. It was also a little faster and could hold more fuel, giving it a longer range. VIIBs carried fourteen torpedoes.

All U-boats had an insignia; U-48's was a black cat. And like all other U-boats in the Kriegsmarine, U-48 carried a full-size German flag: red, with a black swastika encircled by white. The submarines would fly their flags heading back into port.

During the course of the Second World War, the VIIB submarines performed well for the Germans—torpedoed a lot of ships—and this

particular U-boat would go on to be the most successful in the German fleet. In its two years of active service, U-48 would sink fifty-four
merchant ships and one warship, under three different commanders.
Ajax Bleichrodt was about to make his first major contribution to
that record.

Ajax was short and square, handsome, with dark hair. He was
outgoing, talkative, and a hard drinker. He had a good reputation and,
most important, was respected and liked by his crew. Rolf Hilse, the
eighteen-year-old wireless radio engineer on the boat, was struck
by his new commander's confidence and friendliness.

Good morning, Captain, Rolf had said on Bleichrodt's first morning on the boat. Don't call me Captain, Bleichrodt told him. Just tip

Heinrich "Ajax" Bleichrodt. [Wikimedia Commons]

your hat to me when you see me in the morning and when you go to bed at night. Hilse and Bleichrodt became friends during the time they served together on U-48.

The commander didn't have to become friends with everyone, but it was essential for him to have his men's confidence and respect. Admiral Karl Dönitz, creator of the submarine fleet and later the commander in chief of the Kriegsmarine, described the crew of a submarine as a *Schicksalsgemeinschaft*, a "community bound by fate." Each sailor held every other sailor's life in his hands. And the boat's soul was the commander. If the men trusted their leader, they would obey his orders without question. This was imperative while on active patrol. If a U-boat crew didn't follow orders, there easily could be a disaster. There was so much risk, so much at stake. One wrong move, one disobeyed order, and they could all die. An unclosed valve could result in water pouring in, the whole crew drowning; a sudden pressure change also could kill everyone. If a sailor on lookout missed an enemy ship or plane, the U-boat could be destroyed by a depth charge. Each man's role was essential, and everyone had a part in keeping the crew safe and alive.

Even just everyday life on a U-boat depended on cooperation and camaraderie. In U-48, thirty-eight men lived together in a cylindrical hull—with all the equipment for the boat, the bunks, the bathroom, the kitchen, the food, the wireless radio, and, at least to start with, fourteen torpedoes. This space was 160 feet long and only about 15 feet across. In these tight quarters, the men worked, cooked, ate, slept, talked, read—though Rolf thought the light wasn't really good enough for reading—played cards, chess, checkers, and dominoes, listened to music, and went to the bathroom. Once in a while they bathed.

Each crew member had eight hours of sleep, eight hours on watch, and eight hours of standby. When he wasn't standing watch, Rolf

Hilse was "bored sick." Sometimes even being on watch was boring. Rolf could spend hours listening to the radio for ships nearby and hear nothing. Other crew members would look through the periscope while under the water, and through binoculars while on the surface; usually there was nothing to see: days and days with no ships in sight. There were also days and days when the ocean was too wild to fire *die Aale*, "the eels," as they called the torpedoes. If there was no action, there was only a feeling of endless time.

Other than the danger and the boredom, the biggest downside of being in a submarine was the stench. The odor—from old cooking oil, toilets, people vomiting from seasickness, and body odor from three dozen men who couldn't wash very often (and then with only a half gallon of water)—was awful. The men doused themselves liberally with cologne, especially one called 4711, to try to mask the smell. It didn't work.

There was one unbeatable upside to being on a U-boat: the food. Just like the passengers on the *City of Benares*, the crew of U-48 were very well fed, and happy about it. There were sausages hanging between the torpedoes, bacon, ham, cured half boars, venison. Throughout the war, even when food was scarce in Germany, U-boat crews had plenty to eat.

Like most U-boats at that time, U-48 was crewed by young men. Many were still teenagers like Rolf Hilse. The average age of a U-boat sailor was twenty years old. That meant they were always hungry. (Unless they were seasick.)

These young men might or might not have agreed with all that Hitler stood for—murdering Jews, homosexuals, Romany people, and others that *der Führer* ("the leader," as Hitler was known) decided were not "pure" enough to live. But they were fighting for their country, which was Germany. And under Hitler, Germany was trying to take over the world, killing whoever got in the way. U-boat crews' orders were to torpedo as many ships as they could—sink the vessels, destroy the supplies, kill everyone on board.

Rolf Hilse came from a family that was anti-Nazi. His father was vehemently against Hitler. But Rolf had been drafted when he was seventeen and put into U-boat service, mostly because he was under five foot eight and could swim. In the Kriegsmarine, he learned how to write messages in Morse code and how to operate a wireless radio.

Soon after his first stint at sea, just after the war started in 1939, Rolf Hilse actually met Adolf Hitler. Rolf's U-boat had successfully sunk a British battleship and was invited to Berlin to meet *der Führer*. Hitler shook hands with everyone.

When he reached Rolf Hilse, Hitler said to him, I hear you are the baby of the crew.

Yes, *mein Führer*, I am, the seventeen-year-old answered.

How was your experience on the U-boat? Hitler asked him.

I can't remember really a lot, Hilse told him. I was too frightened. Hitler smiled and walked on. The U-boat crew sat down for a celebratory tea.

After a few minutes, Hitler announced, You will excuse me. I am a very busy man. I have to leave.

But before he left, he came back to Rolf, tapped him on the shoulder, and said, I was out in the First World War. I was frightened as well. It will be better next time.

He seemed like such a nice, normal man, Hilse later said.

ON SEPTEMBER 17, 1940, about a year after meeting
Hitler, Rolf Hilse was more experienced, but preparing for an attack
was still suspenseful and scary. On his many missions, he was at the
center of everything—his radio post was next to the commander,
just below the U-boat's conning tower, which held the periscope.

U-48 still had the lead ship in the convoy in its sights. It wasn't
obvious what kind of ship it was. But it was big, and big mattered.

Well, we've got it, Commander Bleichrodt and his crew agreed,
though everyone was tense.

They knew they should be able to sink this ship and get away
without danger to themselves. The lack of a warship with the convoy
made it much less of a risk. But Bleichrodt decided he would wait
until nightfall. Maybe the storm would have abated by then, too.

CHAPTER 8

September 17, 1940

ICY RAIN PELTED the SS *City of Benares*. High winds and enormous waves rocked the ship violently. No passengers were outside, since Captain Landles Nicoll had issued orders for everyone to stay belowdecks. With the turbulent seas and gale-force winds, it would be far too easy for a person to fall overboard into frigid, fatal waters.

Many of the passengers were so seasick, again, that they had no choice but to lie on their beds and groan—or vomit.

Derek Bech stayed in bed all day. The cabin steward, one of the Indian crew, kept checking on him, sweetly trying to get Derek to eat something. But Derek was too seasick and couldn't eat anything.

Down below, the CORB children stayed in their cabins playing cards and reading—except at mealtime. Bess Walder was a little seasick, but not as bad as her roommates. She stayed in her cabin and read, and took care of Ailsa and Patricia. When she saw her little brother, Louis, that day at lunch, she discovered he wasn't nauseated at all.

She went to the rail to breathe in fresh air, hoping that would make her feel better. Louis came over, eating a quarter-pound bar of Cadbury's chocolate, and started waving it in her face. Don't you want a piece? he teased her.

No, she did not!

Then he started eating a succulent orange, which made Bess feel even worse. She was truly annoyed with him.

John McGlashan, the second engineer of the *Benares*, was annoyed, too. But he was angry about something more consequential than obnoxious younger brothers. McGlashan had crewed this ship since its first voyage four years earlier, and as the second in command in the engine room, he knew it could go fast. He agreed with his captain. He thought the ship *should* go fast, and *now*. He knew that if it were up to Captain Nicoll, the convoy would disperse at noon. He agreed with that. So when the convoy stayed together, he was furious. The ship should sail to safe waters quickly. He told the chief engineer that the *Benares* should "cut and run for it." But it did not. The *Benares* stayed with the convoy, continuing to zigzag.

....

JUST BEFORE THE END OF DAY, the rain stopped, the wind died down, and the ship steadied. What a relief to have a lull in the storm.

A few adults strolled the deck, breathing in sea air, grateful for the calm. Some children came out of their cabins to play, too, on their deck below.

The air was storm-cold and damp, the sky rainy grey. Then for a few moments the clouds parted, and the sun appeared. The rays caught water droplets still clinging to the breeze, and in the sky above the SS *City of Benares*, a rainbow appeared.

IN THE DINING ROOM at dinnertime, the passengers were cheerful when they heard the Royal Navy escort had left. They thought that meant they were in safe waters. It felt like a party again.

Those children who weren't seasick ate like kings and queens, just as they had for the past five days. As usual they were allowed more than one dessert, and any flavor of ice cream they wanted. Though the children didn't know this, the more they ate, the better their chances of survival in the cold North Atlantic. For some of them, especially the small ones, it would mean the difference between life and death over the next twenty-four hours. But nobody was thinking about that. They were just enjoying the food.

When their dinner was over, Mary Cornish, Michael Rennie, Sybil Gilliat-Smith, and the other escorts took the CORB children down to their cabins. Mary made sure Gussie, Violet, and Connie Grimmond and her other girls got ready for bed. For the first time since they had boarded the ship, the children were allowed to put on their pajamas. Up until now, they'd been instructed to sleep in their clothes—warm clothes, not pajamas—in case the ship was torpedoed and they had to evacuate quickly. But tonight it was pajamas for everyone.

After Auntie Mary got her girls settled, she went back up to the dining room for her own dinner. She stayed for a while, lingering over a cup of coffee. The wind and rain had started up again. The ship stopped zigzagging because of the weather.

But when there was another lull, around nine thirty, Mary headed outside with her new friend Marjorie Day, the head escort. Sybil Gilliat-Smith, the artist who'd organized the drawing contest, joined them a few minutes later.

Mary wore a thin silk blouse, a thin skirt with a petticoat underneath, and silk stockings. She had on a lightweight, short-sleeved jacket. She was cold, but it was so nice to be outside. The three friends enjoyed the ocean breeze, strolling and talking together.

They talked mostly about the children in their care. There were so many children on board, nobody could know all of them. But the escorts were already quite attached to the children in their own groups, even though they had met them only days earlier. In her group Mary had not only Gussie, Violet, and Connie Grimmond but also two sisters from Sunderland, and another pair of sisters from Middlesex. One of her girls, Marion Thorne, Mary for short, had an older brother, Rex, on board. The youngest girl in Mary's group was a little one called Ann Watson, who had a mass of blond corkscrew curls. The oldest was an artist named Rosemary Spencer-Davies, who at fifteen was, Mary thought, already a beautiful young woman, inside and out. There was also ten-year-old Maureen Dixon, whom Mary described as small and scrappy, with a zest for living. And Eleanor Wright, thirteen, who was always ready to help with the younger children.

Some of the other passengers strolled the deck, too, including a Polish businessman, Bohdan Nagorski, and a friend of his, a diplomat also from Poland. Nagorski and his friend didn't talk to Mary and her friends, but very soon, Bohdan Nagorski would get to know Mary very well.

Mary, Sybil, and Marjorie continued to stroll and chat. Now and again the moon poked out from behind the clouds, shining bright and round, one day past full.

Mary had a lovely voice, and she started to sing. She sang "Greensleeves" because her girls loved it so. The others joined her, and together they sang Christmas carols, anticipating the holiday, three months away. The CORB children would be settled in Canada by Christmas. That was the plan. But in wartime, plans are all too often thwarted. By the next day, just two of these three women would be alive.

NOT FAR AWAY, the German U-boat crew was getting ready to launch their attack. The storm had died down. It was dark. Through the periscope, they had the convoy in view. The lead ship was in good range.

A few minutes before 10:00 p.m., Ajax fired two torpedoes: *Torpedos los!* (Torpedoes away!)

They both missed the ship.

Nobody in the convoy noticed.

....

MARY SAID GOOD NIGHT to Marjorie and Sybil and headed downstairs to her cabin.

On the U-boat, Ajax decided to give it one more shot.

He fired again, at 10:01 p.m.

And in 119 seconds—

....

JUST AS MARY reached the end of the hall leading to the children's quarters, she heard a thud. It was 10:03. The ship shuddered and shook. The lights went out.

Mary was plunged into complete darkness.

She heard glass crashing, wood splintering.

Alarm bells started ringing.

She knew it could be only one thing. What everyone feared had happened.

She had to get to her children.

....

CHAPTER 9

It's Only a Torpedo

DOWN ON THE LOWEST deck, the CORB children woke with a start, some just from the thwack of the torpedo, others from furniture crashing on top of them or water rushing into their cabins. Some children were killed instantly, though nobody would ever know how many. Others were injured from falling debris, some of them so seriously that they would not recover.

A loud bang woke nine-year-old Jack Keeley. Then he heard the alarm bells. He jumped out of bed, quickly put on his boots, not taking the time to put on socks first. He'd slept in his pajamas and did not put on clothes or even his coat. He grabbed his life jacket and ran into the corridor. There was a terrible mess: shards of glass, broken furniture, and other pieces of the ship spewed out from the explosion.

His sister, Joyce, was on the girls' side of the ship. Was she awake, too? As Jack made his way through the hallway, stepping on broken glass and wood, his senses were assaulted. The noise was

overwhelming: the loud alarm bells, more glass shattering, and people screaming and shouting.

There was a dense blue haze filling the air and a terrible acrid odor. It was cordite, used to make explosives, bombs, torpedoes.

Jack ran quickly up the stairs to the upper decks. He knew exactly what he was supposed to do: go to his muster station and get into his assigned lifeboat. Joyce should be doing the same.

....

IN HIS CABIN, Fred Steels had been asleep in the bottom of a bunk bed; the top bunk was empty.

When the torpedo hit, the upper bunk fell on him. Water from burst pipes came pouring in, soaking him as he struggled to get out from under the collapsed bed. He managed to squirm free. He knew he had to get out quickly. The caul his mother had sold to the skipper wouldn't protect him now.

He woke up one of his roommates, Paul Shearing, eleven, who had slept through the explosion. Their other roommate was sitting up in bed crying and looking for his glasses.

Get out of bed, come on, Fred told the boy. But he just kept looking for his glasses.

Paul got his life jacket, and he and Fred tried to get out of the cabin, but the door was stuck. As they pushed and pulled, they urged the other boy to come with them. But the boy didn't move. Finally the door unjammed. Come on, they told him, but he didn't. Fred and Paul ran into the hall. They never knew whether their roommate found his glasses or even managed to get out. He did not survive the night.

In the hall, the alarm bells sounded to Fred like the very devil; the noise was so loud, it made his ears hurt.

He remembered that they'd been told that if they got torpedoed, at least they had the naval escorts to pick them up. But he didn't know the warships had left many hours earlier or that the ships in the convoy were dispersing at this very moment. All but one, that is, the SS *Marina*, a freighter.

At 10:05, the freighter's bridge sent a message to its crew that the SS *City of Benares* had been torpedoed and the convoy was being attacked. The captain called "all hands at once." The *Marina* stayed to see whether it could help. But on the submarine, Ajax Bleichrodt had another idea.

. . . .

ON U-48, THE CREW congratulated themselves. They had no idea there were children on board. This had been a real victory. German U-boat commanders competed with each other over how many tons they sank—and the *Benares* was over eleven thousand tons. Ajax and his crew were thrilled that it was such a big ship. A few of the crew members went up into the conning tower to see what was going on. They saw that the ship was on fire and already sinking.

"We watched the lifeboats going down," Rolf Hilse later said. The crew cheered. But Ajax silenced them. There was another ship they could hit. The minute they saw people going into lifeboats, they went after the next target.

Six minutes after they hit the *Benares*, Ajax and his crew torpedoed the *Marina*. The torpedo hit in forty-three seconds, Rolf Hilse noted in his log, another five thousand tons.

. . . .

AS SOON AS THE TORPEDO HIT, the crew of the *Marina* got into their two lifeboats. But only one of the boats went down well. The other experienced a lot of trouble, landing badly and filling partway with water. This lifeboat would end up alone at sea for eight days until it met a small vessel bound for Glasgow.

The properly launched lifeboat stayed close to the scene of the disaster. This would both help and hurt the passengers of the *Benares*. For some it would mean rescue. For others it would mean confusion that led to abandonment. For when help finally arrived, the extra lifeboat led to a miscount, and one lifeboat with three dozen survivors of the *Benares* would be missed.

....

BACK IN THE CHILDREN'S SECTION, everyone was trying to get out. There was a huge hole where the torpedo had struck, and water was pouring in.

Johnny Baker and his older brother, Bobby, had been fast asleep. They woke when the alarm bells started ringing and quickly got out of their cabin and headed for their muster station. They moved so quickly that little Johnny forgot his life jacket, but he didn't think of it then. He just ran. Fast, as usual. Bobby made sure to stay with him this time.

....

THE SICK ESCORT, Father Rory O'Sullivan, was in a very deep sleep because the doctor had given him a sleeping pill. When the torpedo hit, the explosion threw him out of bed. Afterward he lay on the floor listening to the cracking of splitting wood. The cupboard,

table, chairs, and a mirror had all crashed to the floor and were in a heap around him.

In a drugged and leaden state, he pulled himself up and walked around the dark cabin, looking for his raincoat and his life jacket. He managed to find them, but his feet got cut up walking on broken glass. He couldn't find his flashlight—or any clothes or shoes. He pulled and pulled at the door, but it was stuck. He couldn't get out! After what seemed like an eternity, he finally realized he was pulling at the door of his wardrobe, not the cabin.

When he found the right door, it was actually ajar—some of his boys had opened it for him. And there were boys still in the corridor. He would try to help them get to their boats.

....

THE FURNITURE IN Bess Walder's cabin rocked violently and smashed to the floor when the torpedo hit; she was shaken right out of her bed. Lying there, she could smell oil and the acrid odor of cordite. Then she heard louder and even more terrifying bangs. Bess knew immediately what had happened. So did her roommates, Ailsa Murphy and Patricia Allen. They were wartime children, after all, Bess would say later. And of course, on the *Volendam* Patricia had faced this same thing. She had survived that torpedo strike; all the kids had. That was very reassuring.

Bess took charge of the two younger girls. She made sure they got dressed quickly, which wasn't easy in a dark, crowded cabin. It was terribly hard to maneuver through all the toppled furniture. Bess grabbed her heavy green bathrobe. Her beloved ratty robe.

Was it just a week ago she had argued with her mother about bringing this very robe?

Mrs. Walder had come home from a shopping trip all happy with a surprise: a flowery, lightweight dressing gown. Now you can have this for going away, Bess, her mother had said proudly. You can't take your old one. It's a disgrace.

Bess knew her mother had had to use precious ration coupons to buy the new robe. But she didn't care; she didn't like it. She stamped her foot and said, No! She wanted to take her old familiar robe—a bright green one with nice deep pockets. Sure, it was itchy because it was wool, but she didn't mind. It was warm, and she was comfortable in it, and it was *hers*.

She'd won that battle. And so now, amid the ringing alarm bells and the smell of cordite and smoke—was there fire, too?—Bess put on her old, warm, bright green woolen robe. And over it she put her life jacket.

She made sure that Ailsa and Patricia put on their life jackets, too. These weren't fitted kapok ones, but the big, cumbersome ones with huge cork panels in the back and front. The cork swelled up in the water and kept you from going under. That would come in handy later, but now they were unwieldy. Once the girls had them on, it was even more difficult to move, the three of them in those big cork life jackets, with furniture tumbled all around.

Bess got Patricia out of the cabin and sent her upstairs to the lifeboats. Patricia had been through this before; she would know what to do. But when Bess went back for Ailsa, she couldn't get into the cabin. Something was blocking the door. She grabbed something— she didn't even know what—and made a big enough hole in the door to crawl through.

Ailsa had fallen and was bleeding a lot. Bess was afraid she was bleeding to death.

She had to get herself and Ailsa out of there! In the time it took her to reach Ailsa and move back toward the door, the furniture had shifted, and the wardrobe was blocking the way. It was too heavy for Bess to move. She banged and banged on the wardrobe.

But would anyone hear her over the ringing alarm bells, the shattering glass, and other people yelling?

....

ALL OVER THE SHIP, crew members were working to save passengers. They were getting the lifeboats ready to be launched and helping people into them. After this was all over, the senior surviving officer would issue commendations, including one to captain's boy Abdul Subhan for his heroism, for "his devotion to duty at the launching of the boat, assisting Passengers at the boat and again whilst in the boat." Abdul was cheerful and positive during the crisis. Sadly, he died of exposure before rescue arrived.

Some of the crew were searching for people belowdecks, trapped in their cabins or behind debris in the corridors. Especially the CORB children, whose section of the ship had been devastated by the torpedo. Captain Nicoll and Admiral Mackinnon were directing it all.

The worst had happened, the thing Nicoll had desperately tried to avoid, and now the captain was determined to save his passengers. He knew how bad the damage was. He knew the *Benares* was going down fast. His crew had to get everyone into lifeboats immediately. Especially the children.

Of course, help from the Royal Navy was on the way, but when it would arrive was impossible to say. When the torpedo struck at 10:03, the ship's radio operators had sent out a coded SOS. The message reached a Royal Navy station in Scotland at 10:06. By 10:30, the commander of the navy's Western Approaches office in Liverpool, which monitored activity in the North Atlantic, had the decoded message: the SS *Benares* had been hit by a torpedo. CORB children were on board. Help had to be sent with *utmost dispatch*.

The *Winchelsea*, the destroyer that had left the *Benares*'s convoy, was the closet Royal Navy ship. It could have turned around and rescued the *Benares* passengers. But the Western Approaches commander decided to keep the *Winchelsea* on its mission, escorting a convoy coming from Canada carrying vital supplies for the war effort. Earlier in the day, the *Winchelsea* had rescued the captain and crew from the British merchant *Crown Arun*, a straggler from an incoming convoy that had been torpedoed.

The Western Approaches commander instead tapped HMS *Hurricane*, another destroyer, which was leading Convoy OB-214 out from England toward Canada.

The *Hurricane* was farther away than the *Winchelsea*, about three hundred miles from the scene of the disaster. In good weather, at maximum speed, it would take more than seven hours to reach the *Benares*'s last known location. With the bad weather, it would take even longer. Still, the Western Approaches commander decided the *Hurricane* was the best option.

Western Approaches sent a message to the *Hurricane*. When it reached the *Hurricane*'s radio room, the young telegraphist yelled, "One for us." "CITY OF BENARES TORPEDOED." It gave the location—N 56.43 W 21.15—and said "PROCEED IMMEDIATELY. BEST POSSIBLE SPEED."

Utmost dispatch.

The captain of HMS *Hurricane* was Lieutenant Commander Hugh Crofton Simms. He had a one-year-old son at home. When he saw the words *best possible speed*, he knew that meant women and children were on board. He didn't know yet how *many* children. He didn't know there were *one hundred* children on that ship. But he knew he had to get there fast.

IN THEIR CABIN, Bess banged and hammered on the door, crying out. The room was filling with water. Ailsa was still bleeding profusely.

....

ON THE *HURRICANE* Simms considered his options. The problem was the weather. How fast could he make his ship go in a storm with winds that raged up to fifty miles per hour? The faster he sailed, the more he put the lives of his crew in danger. He had to keep his ship upright and water-free. Of course, he knew that if the weather was bad where he was, it was likely to be bad where the survivors of the *Benares* were, presumably in open, exposed lifeboats. In the cold of the North Atlantic. In a storm. And children would not survive long in such conditions . . .

Best possible speed.

Erring on the side of caution, Simms upped his speed from twelve knots to only fifteen (about seventeen miles per hour) until—and if—the weather got better. Then he would go faster. He wanted to get there as quickly as he could. But he had to actually get there.

....

HELP! BESS YELLED. WE'RE IN HERE!

Finally she heard something on the other side. *Thwack, thwack* . . . It was someone with a hatchet.

She stood back as the crewman made a hole in the door. Bess wrapped her coat around Ailsa and helped her out of the cabin. Luckily one of the escorts came by and took the ten-year-old in her arms. Bess could see Ailsa was doing very poorly, but she was being so brave.

Beth Cummings was in the hallway also, having troubles of her own. Her roommate Joan Irving was hurt badly. Though Beth and Bess couldn't see any blood, Joan couldn't move. Bess helped Beth drag Joan along. They had to go up to the children's playroom, their muster station.

And yet—when they got to the staircase to walk up to the children's room, it wasn't there. The staircase had disappeared completely. There was no way up. The alarm bells were ringing loudly in their ears. Ringing and ringing.

The girls turned around and quickly walked the other way. They found another staircase. They made it up to the next deck and hurried toward the children's room.

I'll go and have a look, Beth told Bess. But Beth found nothing where the children's room should be. Nothing there at all. The sight— the deck gone, the toys, the rocking horse, everything gone—was devastating.

Beth could see the remnants of the little nook where she and Bess used to talk. Soon that would disappear, too.

The ship was disintegrating.

Huge gaps were appearing by the minute. You could look right down through the bottom of the ship into the sea.

Sailors kept pushing children away from the holes, away from certain death.

....

ONLY MINUTES HAD PASSED since the torpedo hit.

Mary Cornish was still making her way down to find her girls, passing CORB children who were coming up. She was desperate to find Gussie, Violet, and Connie Grimmond; the lovely art student,

Rosemary Spencer-Davies; impish Maureen Dixon; little Ann Watson, with her blond corkscrew curls; Eleanor Wright; the two pairs of sisters; all her girls. *All of them.* She had to get them all safely into a lifeboat.

But when she got down to the children's deck, Mary saw nothing where the children's bathrooms had been. The torpedo had struck just below the children's loos. Blown them all to bits. The hole she saw was the size of a London bus.

Below, the deep, dark abyss of the sea.

More holes were opening up.

She had to find her girls.

Mary kept going, through the hallways filled with collapsed walls and thrown furniture.

Debris blocked her way to the girls' cabins.

She had to get through. No crew were around just then to help. So with her bare hands Mary tore aside the wreckage, wrenching away big pieces of furniture, the splintered wood shredding the skin on her hands. She made a hole big enough to crawl through.

On the other side was another escort, Lilian Towns. Lilian had some of Mary's girls with her, including Gussie, Violet, and Connie Grimmond. Thank goodness.

Mary and Lilian and a ship's engineer worked together to rescue other children from their shattered cabins. One girl was seriously hurt and unconscious, but they managed to get her out and hand her off to a sailor. He would get her to a lifeboat.

All the girls were in their pajamas, and *only* their pajamas. Many of them had been hurtled out of their beds, and there was no chance in the dark and the chaos for them to put on coats and shoes. And now there was no time go back for warmer clothes. With the ship listing and disintegrating around them, Mary and Lilian had to get the girls on deck and into lifeboats.

The girls did not panic. They knew the drill. They had their life preservers. They moved quickly and calmly. But of course they *were* frightened. Mary soothed them with the only thing she could think to say. "It's all right, it's only a torpedo," she told them. It's only a torpedo.

Mary knew all they had to do was get up on deck. They would be put in lifeboats. And there would be crew to help them.

When she saw other CORB children, she urged them, Make sure you get to your muster station. Make sure you keep going.

When they looked frightened, she reassured them, It's only a torpedo.

Mary didn't know it yet, but it wasn't only the torpedo. The storm was raging again, and it was growing stronger. The high waves and strong winds and the tilt of the sinking ship, which was still moving, made the launching of the lifeboats precarious.

The freezing rain and cold wind ripping through thin pajamas made time an enemy, too.

But there was nothing anyone could do except get to the lifeboats as fast as possible.

As she made her way upstairs, Mary Cornish kept repeating, as if in prayer, It's only a torpedo.

....

CHAPTER 10

Fate's Hand

BESS AND BETH and the injured girls made it up some narrow steps to the deck with the lifeboats. Just as they got there, the stairs began to collapse behind them. Were we thankful? Bess wondered later. It seemed as if she was in a very bad dream.

The storm was raging. Rain and sleet pounded the deck. Wind blew strong and fierce. High waves pummeled the sinking ship.

There was very little light. The storm clouds hid the moon and the stars. Now and again flares and rockets lit by the crew illuminated fragments of the scene: a person walking quickly and clutching a bag, the rain pelting the deck, a sailor trying to stop a swinging lifeboat, a sailor carrying a child, people coming up from below frantically looking for their lifeboats.

Even in the dark Bess could see that people were bewildered and confused, running here and there. The crew was trying to maintain order, but it wasn't easy. Bess found her group preparing to get into their lifeboat. The littler girls were shivering and scared. Patricia

Allen had made it there, and she was reassuring the other girls. We'll be picked up, like we were before—you'll see, she told them.

Then emergency lights came on, and Bess could see how bad it really was. The sailors were having serious trouble lowering the lifeboats, which now hung from davits off the side of the ship. With the blowing winds, the raging sea, and the ship already tilting into the water, everything was on an angle. The lifeboats were not level. Adding to the instability, the ship was still moving forward; a torpedo hit doesn't stop a ship dead. Although the ship's stokers and firemen had stopped tending to the boilers, the boilers took time to power down. Even once a ship's engines are stopped completely, momentum will keep a vessel moving, and ocean currents propel it along, too. Unfortunately, the continued movement can cause a ship to sink faster because a moving ship takes on water more quickly than a stationary one.

The crew was working against the wind, the rain, and the ship's movement; most of the time they couldn't see what they were doing. Although their actions would later be questioned, the consensus was that they worked well and diligently. But still, because of the difficult conditions, the lifeboats went down jerkily, slanting and tossing from side to side. If a lifeboat wasn't lowered straight and evenly, it could take on water when it landed or, worse, flip over in the wind, dumping passengers into the freezing-cold water below.

While Bess watched all this in horror, tragedy unfolded right next to her. Her roommate Ailsa, who had been injured and was bleeding so much, was dying in the escort's arms. Ailsa had been so brave, Bess thought, had fought to survive, but now she slipped from unconsciousness into death. Bess watched as the escort lowered Ailsa into the sea and said a prayer. It was the first death Bess had ever witnessed. It would not be the last.

But there was no time to think, to process—Bess learned that the lifeboat she'd been assigned to had been smashed to smithereens. A sailor picked her up and threw her into another lifeboat.

What more could go wrong? There couldn't be any more setbacks, nothing more to endure. She would be safe now, she thought. She was in a lifeboat, hanging by the davits, high above the water—roughly thirty feet—and it was about to be lowered. Beth Cummings had made it into this lifeboat, too. Some of the other girls from her group were there. But it was difficult for Bess to see who was there and who wasn't. Patricia Allen, who had survived another torpedo? The injured Joan?

And what about her brother, Louis? Where was he? Had he gotten into a lifeboat? Watch over that young man, her father had said. She sure hadn't! But what could she do now?

Bess held on to the boat as she watched what was going on around her. She saw people still waiting for lifeboats, some people giving up on lifeboats and jumping onto rafts. She saw other passengers panic and jump straight into the sea.

The bad dream had turned into a nightmare, Bess thought. A ghastly one.

The crew started lowering her lifeboat with the pulleys. She could not think about Ailsa or her brother or about anyone else—because the lowering of her lifeboat wasn't going well, not well at all. The boat was tilting and wavering. She had to stay steady and upright. She had to hold on tight or she would fall into the water.

....

FRED STEELS AND PAUL SHEARING had reached the lifeboats. Fred saw chaos and confusion, a lot of people running around. He noticed some children crying, and the next thing he knew someone picked him up and tossed him into a lifeboat. The sailor didn't ask if Fred wanted a hand; he just picked him up and threw him in. A sailor picked up Paul, too, and put him into the same lifeboat. Other CORB boys were in the boat already, with some of the ship's crew. This lifeboat, number 12, was getting very full.

....

MARY CORNISH STOOD on the deck with some of her girls. She knew these girls would get into lifeboats. But what if there were more children below? At least one of her girls was missing. Maybe she and some others were trapped in their cabins or under debris. She had to go back down. She left her girls, including Gussie, Violet, and Connie Grimmond, in the care of other escorts and went down to see whether she could find anyone else.

Mary Cornish was forty-one, a beloved music teacher. She wasn't married and had no children of her own. Back home she was devoted to her students, and they adored her. Before piano recitals, when her pupils were nervous, she'd gently rub their hands to get the blood circulating and to reassure them, hands on hands. Now she felt acute responsibility for her CORB girls, for all the children on the ship.

On her way down to the children's cabins, the emergency lights came on, just as they had up on deck for Bess. Mary could see how bad it was. More water had seeped in. It hadn't been fifteen minutes since the torpedo hit.

Mary reached a hallway that led to the children's cabins. It was blocked. An officer was coming out, squeezing through the debris.

"I've just been through there," he said. "There's nobody left. Go on deck."

She wanted to keep searching, but the officer ordered her. She had no choice but to believe him and obey. Maybe she could be useful in another way. She climbed back up to the lifeboats, navigating past holes and through debris. By the time she got there, her girls were nowhere to be seen.

Were they aft? She headed to—but the officer stopped her again. He ordered her into the nearest lifeboat, number 12, the one with Fred and Paul.

Mary wanted to find her girls, to make sure they were safe. But when she looked into the lifeboat, she saw a few boys huddled together with no escort. Sick as he was, with the flu or seasickness, and still drugged by the sleeping pill, Father Rory O'Sullivan had managed to get some of his boys and himself up to the deck and into this lifeboat. Then he collapsed on the floor, hidden from Mary's view.

The officer told her to get into the boat. Mary didn't have much time to think. She knew that those boys needed her. She knew her girls were with other escorts and hoped they would be all right.

....

MARY'S GIRLS *HAD* gotten into lifeboats. Sybil Gilliat-Smith, who had been with Mary on the deck just twenty minutes earlier, right before the torpedo hit, had Gussie, Violet, and Connie Grimmond in her lifeboat, along with all the girls from her own group. Homesick Joyce Keeley was with her, too—close to twenty girls in all. Also in that lifeboat were the glamorous filmmaker Ruby Grierson and Margaret Zeal, the CORB doctor.

Mary Cornish climbed into lifeboat 12, a move that, like so many decisions that night, sealed her fate, and the fate of those in the boat with her.

CHAPTER 11

The Middle of the Atlantic

AFTER IT TORPEDOED the *Marina* and saw the lifeboats being launched, U-48 left the scene. In other wars, at other times, the enemy would stick around to help survivors. But not this war, not this enemy. According to Rolf Hilse, it wasn't until a year and a half later that the U-boat crew found out there had been children on board the *Benares*. He said that they were shocked and dismayed, that Ajax Bleichrodt was never the same again. Hilse said that if Bleichrodt had known there were children on board, he would not have torpedoed the ship.

But he *had* torpedoed it, and there *were* children on board. There had been one hundred, and now there were fewer. It was the job of the *Benares* crew to save the lives that could still be saved—adults and children.

Most of the children were in serious trouble. The gale made lifesaving very difficult. The boats were being lowered crookedly, swinging on their davits, tipping one way and then another, people holding on, some screaming.

Also at play were the vicissitudes of fate, human error, accident, and bad luck.

Or good luck.

Johnny and Bobby Baker had made it quickly to their muster station and lifeboat. But then Johnny realized he had forgotten his life jacket.

I'll just run back to the cabin and get it, he said to Bobby. If anyone could get there and back fast, it was Johnny Baker. He had been running all over the ship for the past four days and—

NO! said his brother. This was one time Bobby would not let him go. Bobby held on to Johnny so he couldn't run away. A few moments later, someone handed Johnny a life jacket, and he put it on.

He would never know for sure, but Johnny has always assumed that the life jacket was Bobby's, that his big brother had given him his own life jacket.

It all happened very quickly, John Baker remembered years later. Someone said to him, There's your lifeboat; hurry, get in it. So he did. He didn't know where Bobby was; there was no time to think about it. Then as quick as all that, as the lifeboat was being lowered, it tipped at an angle, stern first. Jack Keeley was in that lifeboat, too. Jack fell into the frigid water. A lot of people fell into the water. Bobby must have. But not little Johnny. He managed to grab the seat and hold on.

A sailor said to him, Grab on to this rope ladder. Don't look down, just get up there!

So that's what Johnny did. He grabbed the rope ladder. He grabbed on, as he later said, for dear life.

The crew moved quickly. Bringing the lifeboat back up to the deck, they steadied it and quickly lowered it back down straight.

Bobby wasn't on the lifeboat anymore. Had he been thrown into the water and drowned right away because he didn't have a life jacket? Because he had given it to Johnny? Had a big wave hit him, causing him to swallow water? Had he lingered in the water, watching the ship disappear from his view? Had he died slowly from exposure to the cold water and air? Johnny would never know. But he never saw his big brother again. Later he agonized that the last thing his big brother saw was the *Benares* moving away from him, disappearing from his view.

Bobby Baker was twelve years old.

After the disaster of the first lowering, losing too many children, the adults on Johnny's boat made sure they wouldn't lose *him*. They wrapped the seven-year-old in sacking and tied him tightly to the seat. Perhaps he fell asleep, perhaps he passed out. Maybe he repressed what happened. He wondered afterward, as an adult, whether they gave him a pill or something to knock him out. He would not remember anything from his many hours on the ocean that night.

....

MARJORIE DAY, THE HEAD ESCORT, who half an hour earlier had been singing on the deck with Mary Cornish and Sybil Gilliat-Smith, was in a lifeboat with thirteen girls, including some of Mary's. Her boat was about to be lowered. She looked over and saw Sybil's lifeboat already being lowered.

Gussie, Violet, and Connie Grimmond were in Sybil's boat. So was six-year-old Joyce Keeley, Jack's homesick little sister. The crew was working hard, but Marjorie could see it was going terribly wrong. Just like the boat Jack and Johnny and Bobby had been in, it was tipping to one side and swinging on its davits in the strong wind. And the waves around the ship were so huge that they could reach the lifeboats coming down, and if a wave hit an unsteady lifeboat—

Marjorie watched as Sybil's lifeboat jerked and hung in midair, partway down.

And then catastrophe struck: a wave hit the lifeboat, hard, causing it to tip vertically. All the passengers were dumped out—from the height of a second-story window, more than thirty people fell into the ice-cold sea.

From her lifeboat, Mary Cornish heard the screams, but she didn't know where they were coming from. She was facing a different direction. Some of the boys in her lifeboat turned in time to see exactly what was happening.

Marjorie Day also had a clear view. She watched in disbelief, helpless, horrified, but unable to turn away as the disaster unfolded.

It was her job to protect the children on the ship, all of them, and there was nothing she could do to help.

Violet Grimmond, ten, and Connie, nine, plunged to their deaths.

And little Joyce Keeley, who had never stopped crying for her mother.

Screams louder than the storm pierced the air.

Ruby Grierson would never finish her film.

Margaret Zeal, the CORB doctor, gone, too.

And Gussie Grimmond. Strong, quirky, strong-willed Gussie. Gone.

Everyone in that lifeboat, gone. Just like that.

....

IN A FEW DAYS the letters from Gussie and Violet and Connie would reach the shelter where their family was staying.

The letters would arrive the same day as an official letter from the head of CORB, which began, "I am very distressed to inform you . . ." In that letter Hannah and Eddie Grimmond would read that all five

of their children on the ship had died. The boys, too—Eddie Jr., eight, and Lennie, five—did not survive the night. We don't know how they died.

....

BESS AND BETH'S LIFEBOAT was still in trouble. It was tipping dangerously at one end. Bess held on tight and sat as still and straight as she could. It landed unevenly, taking in so much water that Bess, Beth, and the adults had water up to their waists. The little children were in up to their necks.

Bess watched as the smaller children stretched to keep their heads above the water. She couldn't reach them. The littlest ones didn't seem like they had a chance. The water was so high that some of them just floated right out of the boat. When a wave came, it filled up the boat even more. And the waves kept coming—high as a house. People couldn't bail fast enough.

There was another problem. The sailors in the lifeboat were trying to move away from the sinking ship. When a big ship goes down, small craft nearby are in danger of being sucked down with it. All around the *City of Benares*, lifeboat crews were desperately trying to maneuver away, using the boats' Fleming gear. Fleming gear was made up of ten levers mounted on the inside of the boat, five on each side, attached to a shaft that turned a propeller.

"The unique advantage of lifeboats fitted with this gear," stated an advertisement for the Fleming hand-propelled lifeboat, was that passengers had "full control of the boat when alongside the vessel," enabling them to easily maneuver the boat clear of the ship's side.

But the crew on Bess and Beth's lifeboat could not make the gear work. The lifeboat drills did not include putting the boats in the water. Yes, the Fleming gear took less strength than oars to move a boat in the open sea. But if you've never operated it before, it took time to figure out. They didn't have any extra time!

Bess and Beth's lifeboat crew finally got the gear working and managed to get far enough away from the ship so their little water-logged boat wouldn't be sucked down with the *Benares* when it sank.

But Bess's ghastly nightmare continued. All of a sudden a huge wave hit their boat. Some of the passengers were flung into the ocean.

Bess's friend Beth Cummings was one of those people. Beth didn't know how to swim. She went down in the water as if she were in an elevator, down, down, down. She passed debris from the ship on her way down. Thanks to her life jacket, though, she popped up.

Somehow Beth managed to get herself back to the lifeboat. She hoisted herself over the side and climbed in. It was filled with cold water up to her chest and was terribly unstable, listing to one side.

The waves kept coming. A few adults were able to grab some children and hold them above the water, but Bess watched child after child drown right in front of her.

The dead children floated away, mingling with deck chairs from the ship, chairs Bess remembered seeing adults sitting in, happily sipping their drinks. Chairs children had played with. Children in life vests floated among pieces of furniture and wood from the ship, and there in the middle of it all, Bess saw the rocking horse from the children's playroom, bobbing up and down on the waves.

Then a huge wave came right at her, and the lifeboat flipped over.

CHAPTER 12

....

The Lounge

WHILE THE CORB children had been rushing to get into their lifeboats, the passengers in the upper part of the ship didn't know how bad the damage was. Some of them didn't even know that the ship had been torpedoed.

Many of them were far from where the torpedo hit. The torpedo had struck down below, on the aft of the *City of Benares* on the port (left) side. Colin Ryder Richardson's cabin was on the starboard side. Just before the torpedo hit, he had been listening to the comforting sound of the ball bearing rolling back and forth in the drawer of the table next to his bed. He could tell by how quickly it was rolling that the sea was rough. The rougher the water, the less likely they would be torpedoed . . . *Click-click-click. Click-click-click.*

All of a sudden he heard a very loud bang.

The ball bearing stopped moving.

He smelled explosives.

He heard shouts.

Colin realized right away it was a torpedo. He had to get dressed quickly and make his way to the lounge, his muster station. He had his scarlet life jacket right there in the bed next to him. (Although he had promised his mother he'd wear it day and night, he'd decided that keeping it handy was good enough.) He immediately put it on, on top of his pink pajamas.

He got out of bed and put on his slippers. He looked at his robe. Did he put that on under his life jacket or on top? He couldn't fit it on top of his life jacket, and he could tell from the noises outside his cabin that things were happening rather fast.

I mustn't panic, he told himself. I must think this through rationally. He also had the ship-issued life preserver, with its four large slices of cork—two on the front of your body, two on the back, held by a canvas harness. Now where did that go? he wondered.

He looked at all this equipment, not knowing what to do. He had to get moving, though, so he left his cabin, carrying his cork life preserver in one hand, his bathrobe in the other.

. . . .

DEREK BECH HAD been sound asleep when the torpedo struck. Having been in bed all day, seasick, not eating, he was not in great shape. He heard a thud, like the sound of being inside a drum with someone banging the outside of it.

His mother, in the cabin with him, had not been asleep but was in the bright blue pajamas she had bought especially for the trip. She knew they had to move quickly. She pulled Derek out of bed and threw him on the floor. She told him to get dressed. They both put on clothes over their pajamas. When she bought those blue pajamas in London before the voyage, she had said she could picture herself wearing them in the middle of the Atlantic.

Over his pajamas Derek put on his school trousers, cap, and blazer; a raincoat; and gym shoes. Then he and his mother went to get Barbara and Sonia.

Barbara had been in bed reading and had just turned out her light. Sonia was already asleep. Suddenly Barbara heard a dull thud and thought, Uh-oh, what's that?

And then she heard the alarm bells.

Barbara stood by Sonia's bed. Wake up, she said. I think something's happened. We better get dressed.

At that moment their mother opened her door.

Oh good, Mrs. Bech said, you're awake. Put on some warm things!

Barbara and Sonia put on warm wool underwear. Barbara put on a homemade knitted sweater. Their mother said not to wear slippers, so Sonia put on socks and sturdy sandals. Barbara put on lace-up boots. They both put on warm duffel coats, camel colored, with hoods. Sonia's hair was in pigtails, as usual. At the last minute Barbara also took her nice pink dressing gown, thinking that it might be useful.

They grabbed their life jackets but did not put them on right away because they were so bulky.

Mrs. Bech made sure she had her special travel bag with her: jewelry, passports and other papers, and the bottle of brandy. She had her money around her neck in a little purse—five hundred English pounds, her starting-off-in-Canada money.

The emergency lights were on in their hallway, and there was a strong smell of cordite. But the Bech family did not hurry. Unlike the hallways in the lower part of the ship, there was no broken furniture, no debris, no missing stairways. They walked to their muster station.

When they got to the lounge, lots of passengers were there, as if it were just a happy night on the ship. People stood around talking or sat in the upholstered chairs. Others relaxed on comfortable sofas.

Many of these passengers hadn't gone to bed yet and were just enjoying themselves as usual. Some drank cocktails, some smoked. (At night smoking was prohibited out on the deck, lest the light attract the enemy, but inside with blacked-out windows, it was allowed.) Some were even dancing. Sonia heard someone say "No bid" and realized a game of bridge was going on as well.

Mrs. Bech took her children to sit at a table. They waited a few minutes to see what would happen, but nothing did. Their mother announced that she was going to go back to the cabin and get a few more things just in case they had to leave the ship. She had no idea that lifeboats were already being lowered, people already dying.

She walked over to a sailor at the top of the stairs and asked, Can I pop down to the cabin to get some more things?

Oh no, no! he replied. You mustn't do that. We must all wait here for further instructions.

And so she sat back down with her children. They waited ten minutes, maybe fifteen.

None of the passengers in the lounge were aware of what was going on outside. There was talk that maybe the ship had bumped into another ship in the convoy. Because all the ships were in blackout, with no lights visible outside, it seemed a possibility.

Rumor had it that the officers were investigating the damage and that probably they'd hear what had happened soon, and then go back to bed.

Colin, however, knew it had to be a torpedo. But he didn't know how bad the situation was, and he was only eleven and felt he wasn't in the position to tell adults what to do.

Suddenly the wind blew open the door from the deck, and the passengers in the lounge could see and hear the gale outside.

An officer walking by the lounge saw everyone inside. What are you still doing here? he yelled. Go to your boat stations! The ship is sinking fast! It's going down! You must all go to your boats.

It was the first any of them knew how bad it was.

....

OUTSIDE, COLIN AND THE BECHS could *see* the situation: the storm was battering the ship. And the SS *Benares* was sinking, the stern slanting hard into the water. They knew they must all get to their lifeboats. Fast. There was hardly any time. Was it too late?

The Bechs made their way to their lifeboat station. But when they arrived, the boat was not there. They looked over the side and saw it bobbing up and down on the waves. There was room for them, but how could they get all the way down there? It would be like jumping off a house.

The lifeboat was still attached to the ship by ropes hanging from the davits. A sailor told them that they could climb down the rope and make it into the boat. But they had to hurry.

Barbara looked at the rope. Back at home, she liked gym class and was good at climbing ropes. She turned to her mother and asked, Should I try the ropes?

Do you think you can?

I suppose I could try.

A woman nearby said she was a gym teacher, but she wasn't going to climb down. Barbara hesitated. She turned to the sailor and said, Shall I try?

Yes, go on, he said.

She tied her pink dressing gown around her neck, clasped the rope, and started down, trying to use her feet to grip the rope. But

she realized immediately that stiff lace-up boots were very different from flexible gym shoes. She couldn't grasp the rope with her feet as she had been taught to do. She had to use her hands to climb down, and that's what she did, slowly, hand over hand. It was really hard not to let go and fall into the water. She kept saying to herself, You don't let go, you don't let go, you don't let go . . .

Below her, the lifeboat was still bobbing on the waves. It was not going to be easy to get herself into that boat. She had no idea how to land on an object that wasn't stationary.

Then there it was, the lifeboat right below her, and she let go of the rope. She landed on someone's lap.

From the ship above, her family saw her make it into the lifeboat. The crew was trying to figure out how to get Derek and Sonia and their mother into the boat as well. The sailors put a rope ladder with wooden slats down the side of the ship. Although climbing down on the slats wouldn't be easy, it was easier than climbing down the rope, and it was certainly worth a try. There was nothing else for them to do.

A lascar got onto the ladder first and told Derek to come into his arms. We'll go down step by step until we get there, he said. Derek climbed into the sailor's arms, and they started down.

From the lifeboat, Barbara, on her own seat now, looked up and saw Derek just as he was being hoisted over the side of the ship. She watched him and the lascar make their way slowly down the ladder. She could see that her mother had tied Derek's school cap on with a scarf, which was flying in the wind. She thought it looked rather funny.

Derek and the sailor were partway down the ladder when all of a sudden a huge wave hit them. Barbara watched, helpless, as another big wave hit them. If the lascar hadn't been holding on to

Derek tightly, the nine-year-old would have been swept into the sea, lost forever. That was the first time Derek's life was saved that night.

The sailor started climbing back up with Derek in his arms. It was too dangerous for them to go down.

Barbara's lifeboat was now detached from the davits and had started drifting away from the ship. The crew wouldn't try to maneuver closer at this point; the *City of Benares* was going down fast. There was now no possibility of Derek and Sonia and their mother getting on the boat with Barbara.

....

COLIN HAD BEEN WAITING for instructions to get on his lifeboat. After what seemed like a long time, his lifeboat came down abreast the ship rail. It was banging backward and forward against the ship's side. Laszlo Raskai had been down below helping to get the CORB children out of their cabins. He had gone looking for Colin and found him here, where he was supposed to be, at their lifeboat station.

Someone called out, "Women and children first." Laszlo picked up Colin and carried him into the lifeboat. They were the first ones in. Once he was sure Colin was settled, Laszlo left to make room for other children. He had done his job; Colin was safe.

Laszlo went off to find more ways to help. He was one of the heroes that night. When he saw children tossed from lifeboats, he dove in to rescue them. He grabbed one boy and swam to a lifeboat. And then he dove from the boat to attempt another rescue. Laszlo Raskai did not resurface. The Hungarian journalist gave his life saving children.

Colin's boat filled up with other passengers and some crew. One of the passengers was a fourteen-year-old girl, Patricia Bulmer. She and her mother were late leaving the lounge. They managed to get into their lifeboat, but it capsized. Pat surfaced and made it to Colin's lifeboat, but her mother didn't. Pat was inconsolable, certain her mother had drowned. (She had.)

Sitting next to Colin was one of the ship's nurses. She took Colin on as her responsibility. But before too long, the roles would reverse.

When the lifeboat was full, the sailors lowered it. Like so many other boats that night, it didn't lower smoothly. When it hit the sea, it filled with water. The front tip of the boat was out of the water, and the very back, but the rest was submerged. Colin saw the oars floating out, oars they might need in addition to the Fleming gear to help them move the boat. He heard people shouting. Colin and the nurse were near the stern. He was in water up to his chest. Pat Bulmer had to stand on the locker in the middle to keep her head out of the water.

Colin knew the lifeboat wouldn't sink—lifeboats just didn't sink! (They had buoyancy tanks underneath to keep them afloat.) But he also knew that he was in real danger of floating out of the boat into the sea. His life jacket, the one his mother had made for him, might be *too* buoyant, he realized. He would really have to hold on tight—which was a problem: he still had the cork life preserver in one hand and his robe in the other. The nurse was holding on to him, but he needed free hands in case she let go. He dropped his bathrobe and the life preserver.

Meanwhile, the boat was so full of water that one of the crew was trying to bail it out with his cap, which of course didn't do anything. Other sailors were desperately trying to get the lifeboat away from the *Benares*. Colin watched as the sailors and other adults tried to steer with the Fleming gear, pushing and pulling the levers backward and forward to turn the propeller.

Colin thought about helping, but he knew he was too small. And the nurse was having problems with her life preserver: it was all up around her neck. Colin's custom life jacket was working perfectly. His mother had been smart to give it to him.

As he and the nurse held on to each other, Colin worried because the waves were coming in one side of the lifeboat and going straight through to the other side. The waves were so powerful, it would be easy for one to sweep them both out.

He needed to stay in the boat.

Although it was too dark to see them, he knew there were people stranded in the water. He heard their plaintive cries:

Can we get on your lifeboat?

Are you in a lifeboat?

Meanwhile, some of the passengers in his lifeboat were talking about trying to get into a sturdier one nearby. Perhaps they could manage to steer themselves toward it?

But the waves were so high, it was hard to maneuver. To make matters worse, the water around them was slick with oil from the ship. And the crew members were having trouble with the steering; there was no way of getting to the other lifeboat. Colin and Pat and the nurse and the rest of the passengers were stuck where they were, in their waterlogged lifeboat in oily water, still too close to the ship.

As worried as Colin was, and rightly so, compared with his new friends Sonia and Derek, he was in a relatively good situation. At least he wasn't still on the sinking ship

. . . .

UP ON THE DECK of the *Benares*, Marguerite Bech was trying to figure out how to save her two youngest children. She had no idea how she was going to do it. The ship was obviously going down fast. There were no lifeboats near them. Her only thought was to walk up the deck to get farther away from the water. The ship was sinking stern-first, so they had to walk to the bow as if up a steep hill. The deck was not only steep but also slippery. It was hard to get traction. The wind was blowing, the rain pounding the ship and them.

Derek and Sonia and their mother held on to one another, slipping and sliding up the steep deck toward the bow. Whether or not she would find a way to save herself and her children Marguerite had no idea. It was very possible she was dooming them all to go down with the *City of Benares*.

CHAPTER 13

A Long Green
Tunnel

IN THE U-BOAT, Ajax Bleichrodt and his crew had made their reports and drunk some beer and were getting ready to sleep for the night, those who weren't on duty. U-48's work was done for the day. September 17, 1940, would go down in history as a big day for the U-boat.

They had torpedoed two ships, the *Benares* and the *Marina*, together totaling sixteen thousand tons. But Ajax and his crew were already thinking about new targets. Out there in the ocean were more enemy ships, big ships, a lot of tonnage—prime targets for their eels. The next day U-48 would sink the *Magdalena*, another three thousand tons, leaving no survivors. But that would be the next day. For now, the battle was over.

For the passengers of the *City of Benares*, those who were still alive, freezing in the North Atlantic, the battle was still raging. Some—like Sonia and Derek and their mother—had yet to get off the ship. If they had any chance of surviving, they had to move quickly. The *Benares* was about to go down.

BARBARA BECH'S LIFEBOAT was steady and very full—with passengers and crew. It had been a rough landing for this boat, too, and it had taken on some water. But it wasn't too bad, and Barbara had on her heavy coat. She was comfortable enough, though the waves kept splashing water into the bottom of the boat. Her feet were wet, the water seeping in through her shoes. She had arranged herself as best she could.

But she was startled to hear cries and wails, children's cries.

Help!

Help!

She was able to see lifeboats tipping and people falling into the ice-cold water. Children falling. She saw lifeboats with children in them. Children? She had no idea so many other children were on board the ship. And now with horror she watched as they plunged into the sea . . .

Help! Help! they screamed.

Jack Keeley was one of those children. He had been in the lifeboat with Johnny and Bobby Baker, the icy rain pelting down on him. He'd been shivering in his pajamas, bare feet in boots.

Then, about twenty feet from the water, the boat tipped, and he was dumped into the sea. Just as had happened to his little sister, Joyce, but he didn't know that yet. She died, but he didn't know that yet, either.

While Johnny Baker was getting back up onto the ship, with the help of the crew, Jack was nowhere anyone could see. He had gone under, plunging beneath the surface, down, down, down . . . Yet unlike so many others that night, he held his breath, didn't swallow water, didn't drown. His life jacket helped him bob to the surface.

He opened his eyes. There was the ship! He was right next to it. And as luck would have it, there was a ladder, too, hanging

off the side. He grabbed the bottom of the ladder and hoisted himself up.

It was a long way up—he grabbed on with his hands, one rung at a time. But just above him was a sailor, also climbing, and the sailor had on a big pair of boots. Every time Jack put his hand on a rung of the ladder, the sailor—unknowingly—stepped on it. Finally, halfway up the ladder, the sailor figured out what was happening. He turned around and told Jack, Wait until I'm at the top, then you can climb up.

Jack did as he was told, and he made it to the deck. Of the sinking ship.

THE BECHS WERE slowly making their way toward the bow when a man stopped them. Follow me, he said. I know where there are life rafts. I'll see what we can do.

He wasn't crew, just another passenger, but they followed him.

All of a sudden there was a huge explosion. Another torpedo? No, the boilers. Smoke and flames. The man pushed right through and encouraged Marguerite Bech to come with him. She didn't want to, but she followed him, and they made it past the fire.

The man was a BBC reporter named Eric Davis.

He led them to where the rafts were on the deck. He would launch them.

If they were to get on a raft, Marguerite realized, they couldn't take everything they had with them. She couldn't take her special travel bag. She chose the items she wanted most—including the flask of brandy, which she put in her pocket. She kept the identity papers, the passports, and the money in the pouch around her neck. She wanted to keep her jewelry, too, but when she took the box out of the bag, the lid flipped open and everything spilled out.

Sonia, help me get these, her mother said. They knelt down and managed to retrieve them all, the rings, the diamond brooch.

Sonia, put this box in your pocket. I have no room for it.

There was no time for discussion, so Sonia took the box—the top had a glass inset, painted with a fancy-looking old-fashioned lady in a peach-colored gown and a big hat with bows, a throwback to a more glamorous life, an easier time. . . . Sonia put the jewelry box in her coat pocket.

Jack Keeley was standing near them. He watched Eric Davis and another man lift rafts and throw them into the sea. They were heavy wood, and it seemed impossible to Jack that one man could launch a raft on his own, but that's what they were doing.

Maybe Jack could get on one—

All of a sudden a big wave came at him . . .

Jack was swept off the ship.

Again Jack went down and down and down and down, losing his boots this time. It seemed as though he went all the way to the bottom of the Atlantic Ocean.

....

SOMEONE WAS CALLING out to the Bechs: Come here! Come down here! A man was standing on a raft, and he was in a uniform.

Sonia worried. She was not good at climbing, but she made her way down the ladder and jumped into the water, near the raft. The sailor pulled her on and helped her get settled. Another woman was already there. Up on the ship, a sailor helped Sonia's mother get down the ladder. Derek made it down and onto the raft as well.

Once they were all safely afloat, Eric Davis jumped into the wild and stormy waves.

I'm going to pull you away from the ship, he told them, so you won't get sucked under when the ship goes down. He grabbed the rope of the raft and swam with one arm, pulling with the other, and moved the raft away from the *Benares*.

I must leave you now, he said, and he swam away. There was no room for him on the Bechs' raft.

Eric managed to get on a raft with another man, a member of the crew, who was lying down, obviously injured. Davis had just settled himself on the raft when he heard screaming.

Help! Help! he heard. He looked and saw a little boy "holding on to a piece of wood the size of a pocket handkerchief."

It was Jack Keeley.

After he was swept off the ship, Jack had bobbed back up to the surface of the water, grabbed on to a little piece of wood, and immediately started yelling for help. And then he saw a raft with two men on it—one lying down, one sitting up. He hollered some more. HELP! HELP!

Eric Davis and the other man pulled him onto the raft.

Jack crouched on all fours, sopping wet, shivering, and looked at the man who'd saved him.

I say, mister, I say, thanks very much.

Jack was safe. For now. All around him, he could hear the screams of children who were not safe.

....

BESS WALDER AND BETH CUMMINGS were struggling to survive. They had been thrown into the water when their lifeboat flipped over.

Bess went down, deep down, through what seemed like a long green tunnel. It would have been easy to give up. Just let herself drown.

It would have been, she thought later, the most sensible thing to do. There were no other lifeboats around. All the other ships in the convoy had left. Chances for rescue that night were nonexistent. The younger children from her boat were dead or dying. She didn't know where Beth was. She knew Beth couldn't swim. She was sure only people who knew how to swim could possibly survive.

Bess *did* know how to swim. She had spent summers visiting aunts and uncles on the Sussex coast. Her father had taught her to swim in the ocean, which was much more difficult than swimming in a pool. She had jumped off docks without fear. So had Louis.

Where was Louis? Was he alive?

Whether or not he was, and maybe more so if he wasn't, she had to stay alive. She *had* to. She kept holding her breath underwater.

She heard her father's voice telling her: When you are in difficulties, remember you are like a cork. Human beings are like corks. When they go down, they come up. Her life jacket would help, too.

But, her father had warned, it's when you come up that you have to work.

And then, just as her father said she would, she bobbed to the surface. It seemed she had been in that tunnel a very long time, but it couldn't have been more than a minute.

Work, her father's voice said to her. Work.

She stretched out her arms to swim. She felt so strong, swimming against the waves, and then soon she touched something—the lifeboat! It was right there, next to her. It was still turned over, but at least she could hold on to it. Better to have an upside-down boat than nothing at all.

As she scrambled up the lifeboat, she realized she had sprained her ankle, so she could use only her arms and one leg. But she managed to climb up the rounded side of the boat and grab hold of the keel, which ran along the center of the boat's bottom. Her body was mostly out of the water, her feet still dangling in the waves. The sea was wild, the boat riding up and down the swells. If Bess could just hold on to the metal keel without falling off, she had a chance. She noticed other people, presumably from her lifeboat, holding on to the keel, too. She saw a row of hands clinging like hers, some of them adults', some children's. But it was so dark at that point, she couldn't see whose hands they were.

Could she possibly survive until rescue came? Could the others? Where were the others?

The *Benares* was still there, but it was sinking fast. Where was Beth? Where was Louis?

CHAPTER 14

Ships Cry

COLIN'S WATERLOGGED LIFEBOAT was so close to the ship that it was bumping against the hull. If the crew couldn't steer them away from the *Benares*, they would be sucked down with it. The crew frantically paddled with their hands, trying to get as far away from the ship as they could. It was ludicrous to paddle with hands in that storm, Colin knew. Human hands could not overpower the high waves and the wind. But they were desperate. They had to get away from the ship.

· ·

BESS HELD ON to the keel and saw a very welcome sight. Beth Cummings had made it to the overturned lifeboat, too. She had managed to swim a little and get back to the boat. Now she was trying to get on. Bess held out one hand, and by hanging on with the other, she helped Beth up onto the lifeboat. Now the two friends clung to the keel together, Bess on one side, Beth on the other.

MARY CORNISH'S BOAT, lifeboat 12, was quite crowded. Not only was Mary there with six CORB boys, but there were thirty or more lascars, a few sailors, and Bohdan Nagorski, the Polish businessman who had been strolling the deck. Mary still did not know that Father Rory O'Sullivan was lying at the bottom of the boat, miserably sick. All she knew was that she had to hold on to the boys and keep them safe. Luckily lifeboat 12 was lowered perfectly. It took in no water and dumped nobody out. This boat had a good skipper, which was—and would be—a lifesaver.

On the boat with Mary, Fred Steels could hear people shouting and screaming. And there was just enough light to see people, dead people, floating facedown.

Looking at the ship, Fred noticed a light moving on the deck, back and forth. He knew everybody should have been off by now; it was sinking fast, the ship's stern in the water, the bow tilting up.

What's that light? he asked one of the sailors. That's the captain, the sailor answered. Captain Nicoll was walking around with a flashlight, trying to make sure everybody was off the ship.

The commodore, Admiral Mackinnon, had gotten into a lifeboat. But when a wave struck, he was thrown out. He didn't resurface and did not survive the night.

But Captain Nicoll intended to go down with his ship.

Fred kept his eye on the ship, and it seemed to be going down in slow motion, and then all of a sudden he saw it dive, and away it went.

Mary Cornish watched the ship go down, too. The lights had gone on, and the *City of Benares* looked as if it were on fire.

Colin missed that moment. Fortunately, the luck of the sea had been on the side of those in his lifeboat. The waves pushed the boat far enough away from the liner that it didn't get sucked down. Colin

heard quite a rush of water and noise, and then the ship slid almost all the way down, with just a bit showing. He turned away, briefly, and when he turned back, the ship was gone.

It was more than he could take in: everything from the ship gone. It wasn't just the engines and the machinery, he thought, but everything that had been there for the passengers: the lounge with the bar, the dance floor, the library, the kitchen, the food, the bedding, the chairs he'd made sail across the deck with his friends, the whole shipboard community. Where that all had once been, there was now nothing.

....

BARBARA BECH'S LIFEBOAT was steady and full of people—maybe sixty. They had managed to pull one person from the water into their boat; Barbara thought he was a sea cadet. All seemed to be going well. And despite her wet feet, she was still warm enough—for now.

Barbara saw the *Benares* tilt up against the horizon and disappear. She had no idea where her mother and sister and brother were. Were they still on deck? If so, that was the end. But somehow she just *knew* they were fine. She thought, I don't believe they would drown in front of my eyes and that I wouldn't feel anything. I can't believe that something as dreadful as that would happen and I wouldn't feel a tremor.

Barbara was right: her family had not gone down with the ship. From their raft, Derek and Sonia Bech watched the ship sink. Sonia thought, Oh dear, my John doll has gone down with all those lovely clothes. I will never see him again. But Derek was thinking about the ice cream.

What a waste of ice cream, Derek said to Sonia.

What a waste, she agreed. All that ice cream. They had lived for that ice cream, and now all those flavors, gone. Lost.

....

CLINGING TO THE KEEL of the overturned lifeboat, Bess Walder heard a terrible noise, like a groan. The ship was gone.

Later a sailor asked Bess whether the *Benares* cried when it went down. Yes, she told him, it groaned. How did you know?

Ships have souls, he told her. Ships cry when they sink.

....

THE GERMAN TORPEDO had destroyed the *City of Benares*. Captain Landles Nicoll, who had desperately wanted to speed ahead, to save the children and all his passengers from just this fate, had indeed gone down with his ship.

The torpedo had been tyrannous and strong. Dozens of people had already died. But it wasn't over yet. The storm was tyrannous and strong, too. And it wasn't letting up.

Beth and Bess, the Bechs, Mary Cornish and the six boys in her lifeboat, Jack, Colin—all those who were still alive had to make it through the tyranny of the high waves, the wind, the rain, the hail, the bitter cold. They had to hold on—and hope for rescue.

CHAPTER 15

The Longest Night

THE BECHS HELD on to each other and the raft. Five people were on a raft that was made for three: Derek and Sonia and their mother, Marguerite; Doris Walker, a woman who had been on her way back home to Australia; and Tommy Milligan, the sailor who had helped them onto it.

Milligan was nineteen, an engineer from the ship. He knew that Eric Davis—though he didn't know his name—had saved their lives. If Davis hadn't swum, pulling their raft farther away from the ship, they all would have been sucked under when the *Benares* went down. They had had five minutes to spare. *Five minutes.*

The raft rode up and down on the waves like a bucking bronco, the wind blowing, the hail pelting them. They had to hold on, but it was hard to keep a grip; it hurt.

The raft was a flat, slatted piece of wood, held together with nails and rope, like a diving raft in a lake. Between the slats were buoyancy cylinders—big, empty, rusty drums. The Bechs hung on by putting their fingers into the slats, but the cylinders kept pinching

them so painfully that they had to keep moving their hands to get some relief.

And the waves kept coming, high white horses with their foam. They could hear them approaching as if they actually were galloping horses. One of the people on the raft would shout, Hold on! And they would try to hold on even tighter. It was like going down Niagara Falls, but over and over again.

Already Marguerite's fingers were red with blood. For much of the time she lay on top of Derek so he wouldn't be swept into the sea by a wave. They could see no other rafts, no lifeboats. Now and then bits of wreckage from the ship came their way, but they didn't see another soul. There was no one to help if their raft could not hold them.

As the night wore on, the rough seas would steadily knock the nails out of the Bechs' raft. They didn't realize it, but it was already starting to break apart.

....

COLIN FIGURED THEY were about eight hundred miles from the nearest shore. Actually they were closer, more like six hundred miles from the coast of Ireland. The ship was torpedoed almost three hundred miles from the uninhabited rock of Rockall in the North Atlantic. In any case, they were too far from land; Colin knew his lifeboat was in trouble. It was filled with water, hardly floating, and the storm was raging. Gale-force winds. His mother had assured him that if they were torpedoed, the Royal Navy would rescue them. He had to survive. So that was his goal. He had to concentrate on staying alive and, if he could, helping others in his boat.

People in his boat were dying. Some were swept out into the sea. Others were dying from the cold, lascars mostly, because of their light clothing. And children. Colin had never seen a dead body; now he was surrounded by them.

Exposure to severely cold air and water lowers a person's body temperature so much that everything inside slows down: the liver, kidneys, lungs. Muscles can't function well when they are too cold, so a low body temperature causes the heart muscle to slow down. When the heart slows down, it goes into an irregular rhythm. And then it stops. So the more clothes you have on, and the warmer you are, the more likely you are to survive. If you are lucky enough to be in a lifeboat or a place in a lifeboat that is protected from the wind, you have a better chance of surviving.

Colin was warmer than most in his coat and special life jacket. At some point he put his hands in the pockets of the life jacket and discovered his mother had put gloves inside. They were string gloves, made not for warmth but for gripping onto things. They should help him hold on. He was a very lucky boy.

But others were not so fortunate. As the night went on, more and more people on his boat died. The dead bodies bumped into the survivors. They had to put the dead overboard. Colin helped when he could, though he was busy taking care of the nurse.

She was cold and terrified. Colin cradled her head in his arms and comforted her, while holding on to his seat so he wouldn't fall into the ocean as the boat went up and down the large waves. The adults looked at him in wonder. On the ship walking around by himself, reading a book, talking to the adults, he had seemed so mature for an eleven-year-old. Now, holding on to the nurse, helping the others with the dead bodies, he was more than just mature for his age. He was heroic.

Colin had not wanted to leave home. The farm at Glan Usk near Abergavenny in Wales was heaven. It was so different from London; the farm had no electricity, so at night they had to light oil lamps.

Colin and his brother, Julian, who was six years younger, would walk through a meadow to the river Usk, which was wide and slow and had a beach they could play on.

And Colin was old enough to help the farmers with their crops. He rode horses and mucked about the farm, getting dirty, wearing "rough" clothes. It felt like a vacation, the farm like one big playground. He loved being independent; he was even allowed to ride his bicycle a few miles into town. He would have been perfectly happy to ride out the war there, no matter how long it lasted. But his parents wanted him to go to America, to be safe, because they loved him. So he had told himself to buck up.

And now here he was holding a dying woman in his arms, surrounded by bodies, being pelted with freezing rain and hail on a tumultuous ocean.

....

JACK KEELEY COULDN'T stop his teeth from chattering. The hail was coming down so hard that it felt like people were throwing stones at him. And the cold was *so cold*. All he had on were thin pajamas and a life jacket. His feet were bare, his boots gone. But he didn't complain.

He was always one for questions. Now he asked Eric Davis, How high are the waves? Eric thought they were over twenty feet. Eric and Jack devised a system of tying themselves in knots so they could stay on the raft as it went up and down the high waves. Because that's what it did, all night: up with a wave, down as it passed, up with a wave, down as it passed. Up and down, up and down.

After a while they found some food. There was a little cupboard in the middle of the raft with tins of milk and ship's biscuits. It was

very hard to maneuver well enough to drink the milk, and it was
pretty impossible to eat a ship's biscuit dry. Ship's biscuits—or
hardtack—are made of only flour, water, and a little salt. They are hard
and dry and don't taste like anything much. But if you can manage
to get one down, it will fill you up.

They succeeded in opening a tin of the condensed milk, but it
was difficult to drink. So thick. And how to hold the can and the raft,
too? But Eric told Jack to drink it, so he did. And he told him to eat
the biscuits, and Jack did.

The other man on the raft didn't speak at all. He had been injured,
a gash in his head. It was John McGlashan, the second engineer, the
man who thought that the *Benares* should have left the convoy and
"cut and run." When the torpedo hit, he had been asleep. He was
awakened by a terrific thud.

He knew immediately that the damage was serious and, jumping
out of bed, put on his shoes and proceeded to the engine room con-
trols in his pajamas.

The water in the engine room was already deep and rising quickly.
In a matter of minutes it was up to his waist. The chief engineer
ordered him and the others in the engine room to save themselves.
The ship was going down.

McGlashan went to his muster station for lifeboat 2, but that lifeboat, with Colin Ryder Richardson on it, had already been lowered.
He turned his attention to lifeboat 4. This was Barbara Bech's lifeboat. He helped many passengers get down into it, using a lifeline
and a ladder. Then he went to help launch the rafts. Finally, with
much difficulty, he got himself onto one. When the ship went down,
he was so close that waves threw him off, fortunately near another
raft. That's how he ended up with Eric Davis. Sometime, in all that,
McGlashan had been injured.

He and Eric Davis had heard Jack's cries and managed to haul him onto their raft.

Now the three of them drifted about in heavy seas. McGlashan was suffering from his injury as well as the cold. He was enough of a sailor to know that it was a race against time. Would exposure get to him, little Jack, and Eric Davis before rescue? He held out hope.

....

ALTHOUGH THE NIGHT was dark and stormy, every once in a while the storm abated. The clouds would part, and the moon would shine. It was only one day past full—so when it was not behind a cloud, it cast enough light for the survivors to see a little bit.

Bess Walder saw jeweled hands in the moonlight. Clinging to the keel of the overturned lifeboat was an elderly woman. She had exquisite rings on every finger.

Bess looked around. Who else was holding on, who belonged to the hands she saw? Beth Cummings, her new friend, was still there, holding on to the keel. If Beth, who had never swum in her life, had managed to swim in the cold, high ocean waves to the lifeboat, she could hold on, too. Right? The two new friends, grasping the keel on the opposite sides of the overturned boat, nodded at each other.

They were big, strong girls. They had some hope of surviving; their body types would help. Being bigger, with extra weight, was an advantage. But it would take more than that. It would take determination, guts, and smarts. They both realized to talk would court danger—if they opened their mouths wide, they might swallow a mouthful of water and drown. So they spoke briefly:

Bess said, We'll hang on.

Yes, Beth answered.

They had made a pact.

MARGUERITE BECH KNEW that Derek was young enough and little enough that he could easily fall asleep and die from the cold. He was at greater risk, too, because he hadn't eaten all day, in spite of the nice man bringing him food.

Children who had been eating well, with food in their bellies, had a better chance to survive the cold, though it certainly was not a guarantee. Those with little protective fat, with little food in their systems, were even more likely to die. Luckily for Derek, his mother was with him, and she was determined to keep him alive, lying on top of him, no matter how uncomfortable that was for either of them.

When he drifted into sleep, she yelled at him. Wake up, wake up!

He didn't know he had fallen asleep, but her yells woke him.

Just a few hours earlier, when they knew they wouldn't get onto the lifeboat with Barbara, Marguerite Bech had seen a young woman huddled in a corner of the ship. Tucked under her was a small girl, her daughter. Marguerite told the mother, There are rafts at the other end of the ship; come with us. We're going to get on a raft. But the woman couldn't budge. She was riveted with fright.

Marguerite held on to the raft and Derek. Sonia held on to the raft. They assumed that if they could just hold on until daylight, they would be rescued.

....

MOST OF THE CHILDREN who made it into lifeboats were little, many of them not dressed warmly. All through the night, they drifted into sleep, then unconsciousness, and finally death.

On Colin's lifeboat, fewer and fewer people remained alive. What if his mother had sent Julian with him? He was only five. Would he have died?

The ship's nurse got worse and worse as the hours passed, and then she died in Colin's arms. For a long time he didn't realize she was dead. He kept holding her, comforting her.

....

ON BESS AND BETH'S KEEL, hands started to let go. Those hands with the beautiful rings, those jeweled fingers, were no longer holding on to the keel.

In a matter of hours—how long had it been? Bess didn't know; time was strange—she realized that only three other people were left: Beth and two lascars, one of whom had tied himself to the gear at the back of the boat. He was still there, but dead, having drowned when a big wave washed over him. The other lascar had managed to lash himself up, too, and he was still alive, but Bess thought he was delirious. He kept praying, saying God's name over and over again. Allah. Allah.

It seemed all anyone could do was pray and hope. And hold on.

There had been one great calamity after another, Bess thought. And then a huge wave came, and she was sure it was the end. It was the biggest wave she had ever seen.

Bess gritted her teeth. Hang on! she yelled to Beth, and as soon as she said it, they were both flung sky-high. They held on to the keel; they couldn't let go, or that would be it. Their bodies were slammed back onto the overturned boat like two sacks of coals.

Then it happened again. And again. And again. The waves kept flinging them up and down, their bodies lifted by the force of the water and then banged down onto the hull, over and over. At some point Beth managed to entwine her hands in some rope, but Bess couldn't get to the rope. So she had to keep grasping the keel, holding on tight, not letting go. Her hands were thin, but her determination was strong. It had to be. She had to get back home to her parents. Her mother hadn't been worried about her; she had always been an adventurer. But Louis . . . Where was he? Was he alive? They couldn't lose both children.

. . . .

THE BECHS DIDN'T know there was food on their raft. Sustenance would have helped keep their energy up, helped them stay awake. Having to hold on kept Sonia awake and alert, but as the night wore on, it became harder not to fall asleep, difficult not to

Sonia rolled off the raft into the water. Down, down she went, the jewelry box still in her pocket.

She woke up under the water.

It was calm, peaceful. Sonia knew she had drowned. There was white before her eyes, and she thought, This must be heaven. She thought, I wonder what God is going to be like.

. . . .

BESS KNEW IT would have been so easy to let go, to fall asleep in the water. But she and Beth, across the boat, kept each other going. Bess knew she had to stay alive to explain to her parents what had happened to Louis. It was her doing that they'd gone on the ship.

She'd come home from school one day and told her mother, I want to go to Canada.

How do you propose to do that? her mother answered.

All you have to do is write a letter, Bess told her.

Oh, what nonsense! her mother said.

But they had gotten the CORB materials, and Bess and her father pored over them. And they applied. She and Louis waited every day to see whether a letter would come.

One day, as Bess and Louis were sitting down to breakfast, their mother asked, What would you say to me if I said you could go to Canada? Bess and Louis jumped up and down like jack-in-the-boxes. Her mother nearly dropped the teapot she was holding, they were jumping up and down so much.

Louis. Her father had told her to look after that young man. She hadn't. She had been glad that she didn't have to run after him on the ship.

But now she had to get home to explain to her parents why she hadn't been able to save her brother.

Grow up to be a good woman, her mother had said. She had to grow up. They were supposed to go live with an aunt. The aunt had sent ecstatic letters saying she'd look after her and Louis. Now it was only her, and she had to survive. To get back home. To tell her parents. Explain.

Beth had to get home, too. Her mother would be heartbroken if she died. The two girls, across the boat, didn't talk much—they couldn't—but if one hung on, so did the other.

. . . .

SONIA WAS IN THE WATER. She felt some hands on her. It was Tommy Milligan, the sailor on their raft. He wasn't going to let her find out what God was like, not then. He pulled her back on the raft, put her on her stomach.

Spit out the water, he told her.

She spit it out.

It was still the middle of the night.

....

ON THEIR RAFT Jack Keeley and Eric Davis and John McGlashan dozed, drifting in and out of sleep. None of them was in good shape.

Eric had spent so much energy rescuing people, he was drained. But unlike his BBC colleague Laszlo Raskai, he had survived—so far. McGlashan's head injury made him go in and out of consciousness. Having fallen under the waves twice, Jack was exhausted and freezing in his thin, wet pajamas. Their small raft bobbed up and down, up and down, and Jack fell asleep.

Then all of a sudden he woke, just in time to see that McGlashan had rolled halfway off the raft. The sailor was about to slip into the ocean, unconscious.

Mister! Jack said to Eric Davis. Mister! Eric woke up and saw what Jack was telling him. Together they tried to pull McGlashan back. He was deadweight; he couldn't help at all. It was terribly difficult, but Eric and Jack managed to get him back onto the raft. Jack Keeley had saved John McGlashan's life.

....

SONIA BECH FELL ASLEEP AGAIN. She rolled off the raft again. She wasn't scared. She knew she would be saved. As before, Tommy Milligan pulled her back onto the raft.

It was almost dawn. They had survived the night.

But when the sky lightened, Marguerite Bech looked around and saw no one, nothing. There were no rafts, no lifeboats, and worst of all, no rescue ship. It became too much for her.

Sonia, she said, let's take off our life jackets and go to sleep in the ocean. Don't you think that would be a good idea? Let's just go to sleep in the sea.

CHAPTER 16

Break of Day

DAWN, **SEPTEMBER 18.** The Royal Navy would come and rescue them. That's what Colin's mother had said.

Pat Bulmer, the teenager whose mother had died, was still alive, but the nurse was dead. Colin, you must let go of the nurse, the others told him. But he knew they would be rescued, so how could he let go of her? It seemed unfair.

Finally he tried, but he couldn't do it. Would his arms not move? Would his mind not let him? Eventually one of the crew came over. Colin was weak; his arms had cramped up. He physically couldn't let go of her.

But others helped, and now she was gone. Into the water they put her, just like all the others. So many from his boat were gone. But they would get rescued, Colin was certain. He just had to stay alive.

ON THE LITTLE RAFT, Marguerite Bech was desperate and exhausted and in terrible pain. Her life vest was digging into her because she had spent the whole night pressed down on Derek to keep him alive. Her fingers were pinched and raw and bleeding from holding on to the slats.

Their one night in Liverpool, a week earlier, waiting to board the ship, they had gone to sleep in their comfortable beds in a lovely room at the Adelphi Hotel. Then, all of a sudden, they had heard someone banging on the door.

Mrs. Bech, a voice said, the siren has gone. You must go down to the shelters in the basement.

So they had gone down. They had to sleep on benches in the Turkish bath. Those benches had been terribly uncomfortable. But this—this was agony.

Wouldn't it be better to just give up? She wanted to just take off her life vest and—

NO, Sonia said to her mother. She had survived two tumbles into the ocean. She was only eleven. NO!

She summoned all her strength and yelled at her mother. NO! On no account. I don't think it is a good idea. I don't. That is a *terrible* idea. Of course we're going to be picked up. Sonia was determined. She had hope, the will to live. What she didn't know was that their raft was breaking apart.

....

JACK KEELEY LOOKED around in the daylight. He didn't see anyone else. No other rafts, no lifeboats. Only a seagull every now and then.

Sir, he asked Eric Davis, are we going toward Canada or England?

Neither, Eric could have said. They wouldn't sail anywhere for very long on their little raft. But he reassured Jack. Back to England, I should think. The real question was, Would rescue come in time to save Jack's life?

....

ALL NIGHT BESS and Beth had been battered every which way by the wind, the waves, the lifeboat. And their big life jackets had swollen up so much that they kept cuffing them under the chin, making their skin red and raw. Their jaws were swollen. Their eyes were caked with salt, barely open.

Bess knew she had to live. She had to get home. But it was so hard, being flung up and down by the waves. She was hurting badly. In so many places. And she was exhausted.

So very tired.

With the daylight she, too, began to lose heart. She looked around and saw nobody else; it was just them, Beth and her, and the lascar, barely alive, and the wide Atlantic. It was, Bess thought, a creepy feeling, like one that comes over you when you are in the country at night with nothing but fields in sight. Beth felt this way, too. It was lonely, eerie.

Bess thought that maybe the smart thing to do would be to give up. She could go back to the green tunnel, and sleep forever . . .

Her tongue and lips were so swollen and encrusted with salt, she could barely talk, but there was something she wanted to tell Beth. She couldn't hold on anymore. Let's jump off and swim south, she managed to say.

Beth was tired, too. So tired. But her mother couldn't lose her. No, she told Bess. I can't swim properly. We can't do that.

Okay, Bess thought. If Beth would hold on, so would she. She *would* get home to her parents. She had to explain about Louis.

Bess is holding on, Beth told herself, and so will I.

They stayed where they were, the two girls on the overturned boat, holding on with their aching hands.

....

IT HAD BEEN light for a few hours. Around ten o'clock, twelve hours after the torpedo hit, Sonia Bech saw something. A sail? The rescue ship?

Look! she said to her mother. There's a red sail on the horizon!

Of course there isn't, her mother said. It was probably a hallucination.

When the wave comes up again, Sonia said, everybody should look in that direction, and she pointed to where she had seen the sail.

....

THEY WERE ALL HALLUCINATING.

Beth saw huge fish jumping. Maybe they were real. Maybe they were close enough to the coast to see cod. Maybe not.

Bess saw trays of food coming toward her. On the ship all she'd had to do was clap her hands and one of the stewards would arrive, and she'd ask for a ham roll and not one but two would be presented on a lace cloth on a silver tray. Now she saw trays of food coming toward her. Silver trays.

Beth saw a ship.

Bess saw a ship.

A ship on the horizon, coming to rescue them.

Everyone saw ships.

When his lifeboat was in a trough, Colin would imagine that when he rose up on the next wave there would be a ship. Oh! He saw one. But it was not a ship. A bit of wreckage? Something else? Down in the trough again he told himself, when you come up on the next wave, you'll have another look.

He was holding on for dear life, as he had all night. It was terribly hard to hold on. The boat was still waterlogged. The water had so softened his skin that he could barely grasp the seat. The gloves his mother had put in his pockets were soaked through, so even they weren't helping at this point. But he could not let go and fall into the ocean.

Out of about forty or fifty people on his boat, Colin realized, only a handful were left. The next wave up, maybe he would see a ship. But he had to stay perfectly still and hang on.

....

SONIA WAS CERTAIN she had seen a sail.

And she had! When they were up on a wave again, the others saw it: a red sail. It wasn't a destroyer, but it was a lifeboat. A proper lifeboat. Not as good as a destroyer, but better than their falling-apart raft.

They tried to get the attention of the lifeboat. If they had known there were flares on the raft, they would have set one off. But they didn't know there were flares, just as they didn't know there was food.

Up on the wave, every ten minutes or so, the Bechs and the others on their raft hollered. Here we are! Help!

The skipper of that lifeboat, Mr. Leslie Lewis, knew they were there. He had seen the raft during the night and had kept a mental note of the location. This was one of the two lifeboats from the SS *Marina*. It was full: there were crew members from the *Marina* and people from the *Benares* they had saved in the night. But there was room for more. It was taking a while because of the rough seas, but Mr. Lewis was determined to reach them. He'd been waiting all night.

ON SOME LIFEBOATS, only a few CORB children remained alive; on others, none. On lifeboat 12, Mary Cornish's lifeboat, all six CORB children were still alive: Fred Steels and his roommate Paul Shearing. Ken Sparks and Howard Claytor, both from the London area. Bill Short and Derek Capel. Both Bill and Derek had little brothers on the ship, but they weren't on this lifeboat. Ken Sparks had a good friend from home on the ship, too, ten-year-old Terence Holmes. But he wasn't here, either.

In the morning Mary discovered Father Rory O'Sullivan. He was awfully sick, in no shape to take care of the boys. It was good she was there; taking care of the boys was her job now. It had been a rough night, stormy and cold. So cold. And hard to get comfortable, with the handles from the Fleming gear digging into her back. At one point during the night, someone passed around brandy.

That morning, the sky was storm grey. There was nothing around them but waves. Every once in a while some wreckage would float by. They saw no other lifeboats. And the waves were quite high, which impressed Fred Steels. Up and down, huge waves.

They were all hopeful. Their lifeboat had taken on no water. It was quite crowded, but they would manage.

Surely rescue would come soon.

Ronnie Cooper, the *Benares*'s fourth officer, captained the boat. He and the ship's assistant steward, George Purvis, decided to plan for more days at sea, just in case. At noon, Purvis gave out everyone's first meal since the torpedo: one sardine on a ship's biscuit, and a dipperful of fresh water from a jug on the boat. He had taken stock of the food and water. He knew it all needed to last until they were rescued. There was no reason to think they wouldn't be rescued soon; Cooper knew the *Benares* had put out an SOS. Help had been called. A ship must be on the way. But still he planned for the worst.

MR. LEWIS HAD reached the Bechs. Climb into the lifeboat! the *Marina* crew told the Bechs, Doris Walker, and Tommy Milligan. But they couldn't move. They were stiff and cold and in pain from their hours clinging to the raft. A few lascars from the *Benares* took Derek and Sonia in their arms and lifted them onto the lifeboat.

Derek was wedged in with the Indian sailors; he warmed up quickly. Someone passed him a can of sweetened condensed milk. He sucked some out of a hole in the top, then passed the can to the person next to him. Everyone was given a ship's biscuit.

Sonia was handed a can of milk, too. She thought it was disgusting that she had to lick milk out of a can that another person had put his mouth on. But she was very happy when they gave her some rum! And she got to sit right next to the skipper, Mr. Lewis, and talk to him. He cheered her up. He was cheering everybody up.

The move to the lifeboat came just in time. The Bechs' raft would have broken apart in less than half an hour. And still no Royal Navy ship was in sight.

....

HANGING ON TO their overturned lifeboat, Bess and Beth whispered through their swollen, salt-encrusted lips. With a few words they promised not to give up.

The day had dawned hours ago. Where was the rescue ship? Or even a lifeboat? Where was everyone else from the ship? Was nobody around? Maybe there was a proper lifeboat? Was that a lifeboat? The waves kept flinging them up and crashing them down. They held on. Beth had wrapped a rope around her hand, but she could still slip off.

Bess was just holding on to the keel with her hands.

How long could she keep grasping the keel?

They were just hands, fifteen-year-old hands.

Up and down they went, the waves flinging their bodies over and over again onto the boat. Their bodies crashing into the hull. The cork digging into their chins. Their skin soft like tissue paper.

They hurt so much, they were beyond pain.

How much longer could they last?

How much longer could Jack Keeley last? Or Colin? Where was the rescue ship?

CHAPTER 17

Best Possible Speed

THE CAPTAIN OF HMS *Hurricane*, Hugh Crofton Simms, had kept the speed around fifteen knots (about seventeen miles per hour), through the night. About midmorning, the winds had died down enough for Simms to increase the pace to thirty-one miles per hour. To be of any help, he needed to reach the area with enough daylight to search.

Simms expected it would take many hours to rescue everyone. He didn't know exactly where the survivors would be or how spread out they were. He knew CORB children had been on board, ninety of them. And other children with families. The survivors would be waiting in lifeboats, and conditions were not good. The longer the children were exposed to the cold, the more their chances of survival diminished.

What Simms and his crew didn't know was just how bad the situation was: That so many lifeboats had not lowered well. That some had tipped over, dumping passengers into the water. That many had taken on so much water that children had drowned in the boats. That most of the children were clad only in pajamas. That children had grown so cold in the night that their organs had shut down and they had died. That many were near death now. The crew of the *Hurricane* knew none of this. But they knew they had to find the lifeboats, and quickly.

With wind and currents, the lifeboats had certainly drifted, probably in different directions. So Simms and his navigator, Patrick Fletcher, decided to use a technique called a box search.

Fletcher knew the last position of the *Benares* from the SOS call. He looked at the wind data and mapped out a twenty-square-mile search area, divided into a grid. Simms and Fletcher would navigate the ship into one square, or box, of the grid at a time, and the *Hurricane*'s crew would look slowly and carefully for specks that could be lifeboats or rafts.

The *Hurricane* also carried a small and steady rowboat called a whaler. The whaler would be used to rescue survivors if approaching them in the destroyer proved too dangerous. The wake from a large ship could easily topple a raft or an unsteady lifeboat. Simms also thought there would be so many people to rescue that an extra vessel would be necessary. Albert Gorman, the skipper of the whaler, and his crew were eager and ready.

....

WITH THE INCREASED speed, the *Hurricane* arrived about thirty miles east-northeast of where the *Benares* had gone down. It was earlier than Simms expected—about one in the afternoon.

He slowed the ship to have a good look. He and his crew saw no specks, no possible lifeboats or rafts. But something, someone, could be hidden by the waves. The captain blasted the *Hurricane*'s siren. Anyone in the area would hear that help had arrived.

Simms and his crew listened for an answer, a horn blowing back, someone yelling. They looked for flares, flags, someone waving a shirt. They looked and listened for any kind of a signal. They waited. Blasted their horn again.

There was no answer.

This probably meant that nobody was nearby. But they had to be sure. Someone could be on a raft or a lifeboat with no way to signal back. This was the first square of the grid; there were many more to go. The *Hurricane* moved very slowly as every available sailor peered through binoculars and telescopes or searched with their naked eyes.

They didn't see any debris, no sign of the *Benares*. The destroyer moved slowly through the entire area of that square. Nothing.

....

MEANWHILE, THE NUMBER of survivors continued to dwindle. Some lifeboats had no live people on them. Some, like Colin's, had only a few. One lifeboat had two CORB boys who would survive only if they were rescued soon.

Bess and Beth and the remaining lascar were weakening to the point of near death.

All three people on Jack's raft were alive, but John McGlashan was drifting in and out of consciousness.

Sonia and Derek and Marguerite Bech, now on the *Marina*'s lifeboat, were alive and comfortable, but they didn't know where Barbara was. Whether she was even alive.

Barbara Bech *was* alive. In fact, her lifeboat was in good shape, one of the few that had landed well enough.

As was Mary Cornish's. Waiting for rescue, Mary was keeping the boys entertained as best she could. Mostly they were talking about what had happened, going over and over again where they'd been, what they'd been doing when the torpedo hit. They asked each other, Would you rather be torpedoed at sea or bombed at home? Torpedoed at sea! was the resounding answer every time.

....

THE *HURRICANE* KEPT searching. Finally someone spotted a sail. They were now fourteen miles away from where the *Benares* had gone down.

The sail was on the *Marina*'s lifeboat, the one that held survivors from the *Benares*—including Derek, Sonia, and Marguerite Bech. Simms navigated the destroyer carefully toward the smaller craft.

The Bechs saw its silver outline.

Even though the ship was moving toward them, Derek Bech couldn't believe the rescue would really happen. After the night on the raft, his mother lying on top of him so he wouldn't fall into the sea and die, Sonia tumbling into the sea twice and being saved by Tommy Milligan, his mother struggling to hold on to the raft, her fingers ripped and red with blood . . .

And then at dawn threatening to give up . . .

Then the lifeboat, food, water, condensed milk, blankets, bodies, warmth . . .

He didn't believe the rescue ship would come, didn't know when it would come, but then all of a sudden, here it was.

The *Hurricane* crew instructed the *Marina* crew to lower the lifeboat sail to keep the craft stationary. The *Hurricane* would come to them. Stay put, sit still.

Derek had to sit still? And wait? It seemed impossible. On the other hand, he did not have the strength to jump up and down. He and his sister and mother could barely move, they were so stiff and sore and tired.

The *Hurricane* pulled next to the lifeboat. When the crew saw Sonia and Derek, they began cheering and yelling. They were thrilled to rescue some children.

Sonia watched as a net was thrown down the ship's side. The crew from the *Marina* easily scrambled up the squares of rope. But Sonia and Derek and their mother couldn't move, let alone climb up a net. None of the *Benares* people could.

The rescuers knew what to do: a sailor entangled his legs in the net, leaving his arms free. The crew made a line of people, passing Sonia and Derek and their mother up the net to the deck of the *Hurricane*.

Sonia felt like a wet sack.

When they put her down, a sailor asked, Can you walk?

Well, of course I can walk, she answered.

She put one foot out to take a step and immediately fell down.

A sailor picked her up and carried her to a room by the ship's funnel, or flue. It's where sailors went to warm up after coming off watch.

As the ship started moving slowly again, continuing the search for more survivors, the Bechs began to thaw out. They were caked in salt from the ocean and needed a warm bath.

Their life jackets had shrunk, and the sailors cut them off. They gave Derek and Sonia warm milk; Marguerite and the other adults were given rum. Once they were warm enough, the Bechs were taken belowdecks.

Sonia and Derek undressed. Sonia took off her coat. She discovered that, unbelievably, the jewelry box was still there, in her pocket, with the rings and brooch still in it.

Marguerite gave Sonia and Derek a hot bath and put them in clothes the sailors had given them—the sailors' own clothes, way

too big, but Sonia thought they were gorgeous, the white and flowing tropical pants and tops. Warm, dry. Heavenly.

They ate hot food—vegetable soup, baked beans.

And then, warm and fed, Sonia and Derek were put in the captain's bed, where they fell fast asleep.

But Marguerite couldn't sleep. Where was Barbara? She could not sleep until she knew Barbara was safe.

....

THE *HURRICANE* CREW was cheered by the rescue of these people, especially the two children. They were determined to find more. Simms continued to maneuver slowly through the boxes on the grid, the crew on lookout all around the ship, at the bow and the stern, starboard and port, in the crow's nest. They saw nothing— just the empty ocean, no lifeboats, no rafts, no debris, mile after painstaking mile—for two hours.

Somewhere out there Bess and Beth were clinging to their over-turned lifeboat. Colin was sitting very still in the middle of his. Jack Keeley was so cold . . .

Finally the *Hurricane* crew spotted some dots in the distance. Could they be lifeboats with more survivors? They sailed closer, and through binoculars sailors could see four wooden rafts. Each raft held only one person, all Indian sailors. One of the men sat cross-legged on the nearest. The *Hurricane* crew rescued the sailors, slowly, carefully, tying a line around their chests and pulling them up onto the ship. It took half an hour to rescue the four. Each one was almost dead.

By now it was late afternoon. There weren't many hours of day-light left.

On his raft Jack Keeley felt a storm coming on.

CHAPTER 18

The *Hurricane*

BESS AND BETH were beyond pain. Their bodies were bruised and battered from riding the waves and hitting the lifeboat's hull over and over again for hours. Bess felt like the front of her body was jelly. They were healthy, well-fed, strong girls, but their bodies couldn't take much more. How could they last through another night?

COLIN WAS IN terrible shape, too, and he knew it. Once again, he recalled that his mother had promised him that the Royal Navy would arrive. But hour after hour went by, and it hadn't. He was so very cold. And immersed in salt water for so long, his skin had become very soft. Too soft. He couldn't use his hands at all.

He also couldn't stop shivering. So many people on his lifeboat had died. He couldn't last much longer either.

REMARKABLY, THE RAFT that held nine-year-old Jack Keeley, BBC reporter Eric Davis, and the injured crewman John McGlashan was not falling apart. For hours and hours it had been riding the waves up and down, up and down, getting bombarded with hail and sleet and rain and salty seawater. Jack's little body was holding up, too, but how much longer? Before he made it onto this raft, he had gone down in the ocean twice. He was barely dressed. He was cold to the bone. He had been cold for so long.

He was still alive against all odds. Looking at the sky, he saw it greying. The air seemed colder.

Or was he dying—?

Sometimes he and Eric Davis talked, but McGlashan didn't talk at all. Jack could see that the sailor was breathing, still alive, but he couldn't tell if he was awake.

McGlashan was drifting in and out of consciousness.

Eric noticed that Jack was asking fewer questions. He was worried about the boy. The quieter he got . . .

And then, late in the day, no ship in sight, Jack asked a question that truly alarmed Eric: How do you stop these things when you want to get off?

Was the boy delirious? Eric panicked. The thought was an ominous one. If Jack's mind was going, his body was, too. He was so little, and so cold. How could he survive much longer? Eric just couldn't let the boy die. But there was no ship in sight. *Nothing* in sight. No lifeboats, no rafts. They were all alone on the vast sea. There was little for Eric to do but wait. And hope. And hold on to Jack.

. . . .

AS THE HOURS passed with so few people rescued, the crew of the *Hurricane* realized how bad the situation was. With such a wide area to search, once they found rafts or boats, would the people on them even be alive? Lieutenant Commander Simms would later describe the dread in a poem he sent to his wife and mother:

> *There's something quite exciting it gives you quite a thrill,*
> *About a fast destroyer and her own free will;*
> *But dead still children on a storm tossed sea*
> *To greet you when you get there is an awful thing to see.*
> *In the cold grey dawn, with the rising sun,*
> *Cannot you now see them dying, one by one?*
> *When the noontide came, and the boats were nearly done,*
> *Cannot you now see them dying, one by one?*

....

SUDDENLY IN THE DISTANCE, Jack Keeley and Eric Davis heard a noise. They'd been hearing noises all day, but the noises had never amounted to anything. Maybe they'd been dreaming them. Yet maybe this noise would be different.

Then McGlashan moved. The sailor had heard the noise, too.

Perhaps, Jack thought, as weak and compromised as McGlashan was, he still knew the difference between an imagined sound and a real one.

On the raft, they couldn't see anything when they were down in a trough. But maybe when they were up again on a wave . . .

And then they *were* up on a wave, and McGlashan managed to utter a word: *destroyer*.

They were going to be rescued!

Eric and Jack and McGlashan watched the ship and then—in horror—watched it turn away . . .

What?

It couldn't be.

Jack and Eric shouted their heads off. How they had the energy it is impossible to know. But as loud as they screamed, the sailors on the ship wouldn't be able to hear them—there was the blowing of the wind, the noise of the ship's engines.

But there was no need for the shouting. They'd been seen. Although to Jack and Eric it looked as though they were being abandoned, the crew was just making sure they weren't leaving anyone else behind before they headed for the raft. It was a calculated decision.

McGlashan had revived with the hope of rescue. He watched as the ship came toward them at what seemed like full speed. The crew members of the *Hurricane* were planning how best to rescue the three on the raft. They were afraid that if the destroyer got too close, the ship's wake would capsize the raft. So they decided to use the ship's whaler.

Skipper Albert Gorman and his crew would be able to get close. They could bring the passengers onto the smaller boat first, and then to the destroyer. Gorman's priority, of course, was the little boy.

But the *Hurricane* beat the whaler to the raft, and the destroyer's crew couldn't wait. They decided to go for it. It might have not been the best idea.

A sailor threw down a rope, and it missed.

Another sailor threw a rope, and this one hit Eric Davis on the head, knocking him back.

Eric managed, even so, to grab it. He held on to Jack. His priority, too, was Jack. Jack needed to get on that ship.

Jack himself tried to stand up, but he couldn't. Then he thought that if he rolled into the water, someone could scoop him up—but Eric wouldn't let him go.

Sailors from the destroyer made their way down the rope. They grabbed Jack. One of them carried the boy up the rope onto the *Hurricane*.

Just then a wave hit the raft, capsizing it. Eric Davis and John McGlashan were thrown into the sea.

But it was not their time to die. Three sailors immediately dove in and rescued the two men. They swam Eric Davis and John McGlashan to the ship.

Later, after McGlashan recovered from his wounds, he made his officer's report, in which he praised the care he was given on the *Hurricane*: "I was by this time in a semi-conscious condition and when lifted aboard the greatest care and kindness for my recovery was shewn by the Navy."

He would take longer to recover than Eric Davis. But Davis would live for only another year or so. He would be killed in a plane crash while reporting on the war.

Soon after this night, however, Eric Davis recorded and broadcast a couple of radio pieces about the torpedoing of the *Benares*. He spoke of his fury at the Germans for torpedoing the ship, a ship with passengers from many different countries: Poland, Hungary, France, Germany, Czechoslovakia, Austria, Iran, Switzerland, and the Netherlands. People who represented "all that was free and hopeful in Europe," Eric Davis said. And of course, he spoke of the children. Davis spoke about the heroism and courage he saw that night, neglecting to mention his own. He told listeners about a young woman who had been rescued, and who managed to keep looking glamorous, lipstick and all, despite the torpedoing and the grave conditions. But the person he talked about the most was Jack Keeley. He told about Jack's bravery and his questions, about his politeness, how he never complained. How he saved John McGlashan's life. Eric Davis was full of admiration for Jack Keeley. And for the crew of the *Hurricane*.

But that would be later. Now Jack was so cold that his life was still in danger. The crew took him straight down to the engine room. The contrast, Jack later said, "was like walking out of an iceberg place into a boiler." Sailors helped Jack take off his life jacket and his pajamas; they wrapped him in a blanket. He got a drop of rum in some water, and he would soon get some fresh, dry clothes to wear and food in his belly.

Meanwhile the ship kept moving; there were more people to save—the *Hurricane* crew could only hope.

....

THE SUN STARTED its slide into the sea. Soon it would be evening and a second night on the water. How could the survivors live through another? Especially the children?

....

AS THE *HURRICANE* moved through the search area, the crew members were devastated by what they saw. Dead lascars on rafts. Dead children in boats. Their captain would also write of this in his poem:

> *There's something very terrible, and something not*
> *   much fun*
> *About the North Atlantic and the fiendish Hun;*
> *A dead stiff on the deep blue sea,*
> *That is very terrible, terrible for me;*

And the cold grey sea and the cold grey mist
Are kissing little children that their mothers kissed.
The devilry of Germans I shall not forget
Seeing little children floating, corpses, wet;
Why were they evacuated? Just to miss
Their fiendishness and cruelty, but look at this.

They needed to find more survivors.

....

"CLINGING ON FOR DEAR LIFE." That phrase was never so apt as it was for Bess holding on to the keel. Hour after hour after hour. It had been almost nineteen hours since the torpedo hit, almost nineteen hours, then, since Beth and Bess had been holding on.

Now Bess saw a small black dot on the horizon. Just a dot.

She'd seen trays of food coming toward her.

Trays she knew in her heart weren't really there. And had never arrived.

So she could not let herself believe the dot was anything. She didn't tell Beth; she didn't want to raise her hopes unduly. Still, she couldn't stop staring at it. She stared and stared, and the dot seemed to grow bigger. Then she saw masts and then . . .

The zigzagging dazzle paint of a British destroyer.

She tried to grab Beth's attention. Her lips could barely move, so encrusted with salt and swollen were they. But she had to tell her.

SHIP, she said. Or hoped she said. DESTROYER.

Bess was determined Beth should understand.

SHIP, Bess said again.

Beth shook her head no. She understood what Bess was saying, but she didn't believe her. She managed to get out the word: NO.

She'd thought she'd seen ships before. They both had. And nothing had appeared—no ship, no rescuers.

No use getting their hopes up.

But Beth kept watching that dot, too, and as it got closer they could see . . . it was a SHIP!

It really was a ship! But was it definitely one of theirs? Or could it be a German ship? An enemy ship? In disguise? Beth and Bess needed to talk to each other. They strained to get the words through their dry mouths, their swollen tongues. It was impossible. But they made it possible. The words came out well enough that they understood each other. They had the same questions, anyway: Was it the Royal Navy? Germany? Even a German ship would be better than nothing. They were desperate to get on a ship. Out of the water. Get warm, get dry. Feel less pain. They agreed.

And as the ship grew closer, Bess saw that it had a great big H06 on its hull. It definitely was a British warship, come to rescue them.

And on that warship, there was much anticipation to save the people the crew could see clinging to an overturned lifeboat. And when they sailed closer and saw that two of the people were children, two *living* teenage girls, the *Hurricane* crew cheered and hollered so loudly that it sounded to Bess like the crowd at a rugby game.

Hold on, hold on, we're coming! Beth heard them shout.

The sailors were ecstatic. And then they saw the third person holding on. The Indian sailor also had miraculously made it through the night.

The crew couldn't celebrate yet. They had to get these three terribly weak and injured people onto the *Hurricane*. This was not going to be easy. The risk of injuring or even killing them was great.

Now was the perfect time to use the whaler. Albert Gorman was ready. He navigated as his crew rowed quickly to Bess and Beth and the sailor.

Gorman got close enough to touch Bess.

Come on, darling, Albert said to Bess. Let's go.

But this darling, Bess said afterward, couldn't take her fingers off the keel. They had been holding on for so long, they were stuck. She couldn't budge them. So Albert Gorman carefully pried off her fingers, one by one, bending them back as gently as he could, releasing their grip. Her fingers were bloated and soft, like jelly. Every time Gorman pulled one off the keel, the skin ripped right off. Every time. Each of her fingers was shredded and bleeding. Bess did not cry.

Gorman wrapped her in a big, warm blanket and lifted her into the whaler. She must have passed out because she had no memory later of getting into the whaler. Throw something down her throat, Gorman instructed one of his crew. She didn't realize it at the time, but what got thrown down her throat was rum. Her mother had been so upset after putting her and her brother on the train to Liverpool that she had gone to a hotel bar for a drink. Now here was Bess, in very different circumstances, drinking alcohol, too.

Gorman helped Beth next, disentangling her hands from the rope and the keel, her skin ripping and bleeding, too. She did not cry either. Gorman got her into the whaler. They saved the sailor last. He was unconscious but alive.

Al Gorman kept a journal, and many years later, when he was ninety-one, he shared it and his memories with a reporter. He said that he and his crew sped back to the *Hurricane* as fast as they could row with these three survivors, all of them unconscious. He had no

idea whether the girls would live long enough to get them onto the ship and into the doctor's care. He had one thought, and one thought only. It was a prayer: Please, God, let them live.

The *Hurricane*'s crew cheered again as Beth and Bess and the sailor were taken on board. While the crew and the ship's doctor began to look after them, Gorman and his whaler crew set off for another lifeboat that had been spotted. That lifeboat was full of people. There were twenty at least.

As Gorman approached the lifeboat, though, he saw that the people were sitting very still. He and his crew climbed on board, knowing that any survivors would need help getting into the whaler.

But the lifeboat passengers did not react. There was a woman with a toddler. A young sailor picked up the toddler and made his way through the boat. Gorman watched. Finally, he had to tell the sailor to put down the toddler.

No, the sailor said.

We are looking for people who are alive, Gorman told the young man. The sailor didn't seem to understand. But finally he put down the dead toddler—and then vomited off the side of the boat.

Gorman and his crew realized with horror that everyone on this lifeboat was dead.

How was it that Beth and Bess had survived and all these other people were dead? No time to think. They had to move on, get to other lifeboats, see whether there were more survivors to rescue. There were.

. . . .

COLIN RYDER RICHARDSON, in his scarlet silk life jacket, was still alive. He was so cold, he couldn't feel his legs at all. He sat in the middle of the lifeboat, waist-deep in water. Waiting.

And waiting.

Finally, after more than twenty hours, the Royal Navy was arriving.

Maybe.

The survivors were spread so far apart, on rafts and lifeboats, that in most cases they could not see the ship rescuing others. So it wasn't until it was coming for them that they were sure. But Colin thought he saw a ship.

It was surreal. It might not be real. He didn't believe his own eyes. He knew that the *Benares* had been in the middle of the North Atlantic. He knew that their own escort would not have come back. He knew that other destroyers nearby would likely be protecting and escorting other ships. But there it was—a warship—and it was coming to rescue him. The Royal Navy had, indeed, finally arrived, just as his mother had said it would.

The people on his lifeboat started to sing.

As the *Hurricane* got closer, the crew was shocked at the sound of the few survivors actually singing. And in the middle of the boat was a small, round-faced boy in a bright red life jacket, sitting straight and tall, shivering.

The destroyer moved alongside Colin's lifeboat. The crew lowered a rope and told him to grab on. But Colin couldn't move. Not only were his hands too soft to hold on to anything, but he literally couldn't move. His life jacket had been holding him in one position for so long that he felt like a statue. It was only then that he realized he hadn't moved at all in hours. He'd been like a human-shaped pillar of stone going up and down with the waves. A Colin statue sitting in the lifeboat.

He knew what he was supposed to do. He knew he was supposed to climb up the rope, get into the destroyer.

But it was physically impossible.

Gorman and his boat pulled alongside and asked the crew on deck to throw down another rope. Then Gorman and another sailor made a kind of harness for Colin, tying a rope under his armpits. Colin couldn't help at all, and so they slowly and gingerly, very carefully, to do no harm, lifted him up.

On the *Hurricane*, the crew hurried Colin into the engine room. They were scared he would die. He could have. But slowly the warmth from the engine started to thaw him out. Some sailors helped him take off his scarlet-red life jacket, now sopping wet and encrusted with sea salt. He took off his dirty, oily clothes. The sailors wrapped him in a towel and gave him something warm to drink.

Looking back years later, Colin was amazed to realize how young the sailors were. Some of the *Hurricane* crew were only eighteen years old, only seven years older than he was. Al Gorman was twenty-seven. The captain of the *Hurricane*, who was considered to be the old man of the ship, had turned thirty-four five days earlier.

Now all Colin could think about was getting warmer—and clean. He really wanted a shower. He was covered with oil from the *Benares*. His lifeboat had been so close to the sinking ship that he had oil in his hair and in his mouth and under his nails. It bothered him terribly.

But first the ship's doctor, Peter Collinson, wanted to examine him to make sure he didn't have any wounds or need immediate medical attention. He didn't. He just needed to get warm and eventually have some food and water. Colin really wanted a shower. Finally he got one, and he felt much better after washing away all the dirt and oil and salt.

He had lived through a horrific night and day, through things no eleven-year-old should have to. Colin Ryder Richardson—who just a day before had been a happy boy, on an adventure, playing ghosts, sailing deck chairs—had lived through it and would be forever changed. But at least he, unlike so many others, was alive.

....

AS THE *HURRICANE* continued to look for survivors, most of those already on board fell asleep. Colin did, just as Sonia and Derek Bech had. Beth slept, too. But Bess was having trouble, worried about her brother, Louis.

Marguerite Bech could not sleep, either. She needed to know what had happened to Barbara. So she stayed awake and helped the crew. As each boat arrived with survivors, she took the few children in her arms, rubbed their limbs, and sometimes even smacked their faces to revive them. With each boat she and the crew heard different parts of the story—how many children had died, how many escorts, how many adult passengers.

One teenager who survived was Tony Quinton. He would later serve in Parliament. His mother survived, too. In a full lifeboat, they were two of only eight who lived.

So many people lost family. Pat Bulmer, on Colin's lifeboat, had lost her mother.

Monika Lanyi, daughter of the famous German writer Thomas Mann, had been on the *Benares*. Her father was living in exile in America, speaking out against Hitler. Monika and her husband, Jeno, were on their way to America. Monika and Jeno had gotten into a lifeboat together, but the boat was damaged during launch, and Jeno Lanyi was thrown overboard and died. Monika survived.

As Marguerite greeted each boat, it became clear what a tragedy this had been. And with each boat, she asked, Is there a girl named Barbara on board?

Boat after boat, there was no Barbara.

And there were many more adult survivors than children.

On the *Hurricane* sailed, through all the boxes on the search grid, the crew desperate to find more survivors.

CHAPTER 19

Phoenixes

JOHNNY BAKER HAD been wrapped in sacking and tied to one of the seats of his lifeboat. But when the adults saw the rescue ship coming toward them, they untied Johnny so that he could sit up and watch.

He was so little, only seven years old, that he kept dozing off and later had only a vague impression of being rescued. He would turn out to be the youngest survivor.

Once he was on the ship, warm and dry, with something in his belly, all he cared about was his brother. Where was Bobby? He must be on the *Hurricane* somewhere, Johnny thought. As soon as they would let him, he would find him. He sure knew his way around ships by now.

Bess Walder also could not stop worrying about her brother. How was she going to explain to her parents that she hadn't taken care of Louis? She had no idea what had happened to him: Whether he got on a lifeboat or not. Whether he died in his cabin or in the ocean.

Marguerite Bech had lost hope that she'd ever see her Barbara again. Have you seen a girl called Barbara? Is there a girl called Barbara on your boat?

The answer was no, over and over again.

. . . .

IN THE LIFEBOAT the *Hurricane* had left for last—because the crew could see it was in good shape—the passengers were eager to get onto the ship. They sat and watched as the destroyer maneuvered here and there, looking for other survivors to save.

Finally the *Hurricane* came alongside.

Wait in your boat, the crew said. Don't move, we'll get you up here. Two sailors jumped into the lifeboat and handed up passengers. They put them around the funnel to get them warm.

The passengers of this lifeboat hadn't been long around the funnel when a head popped around the door and a sailor's voice asked, Is there a girl here called Barbara?

Barbara Bech said, Yes. I'm Barbara.

Thank goodness for that, the sailor said, because your mother's been so worried about you.

Barbara Bech was on the last lifeboat to be rescued.

When the *Benares* sank, she had felt nothing about her mother and her siblings. And so she thought, Well, if they were on that ship, if they had all died in any way, I would *know* it. I would *have* to know it. So they must be fine. Barbara had not been worrying at all.

The opposite, of course, was true for her mother.

. . . .

MARGUERITE BECH WAS overjoyed. She gathered her children together. Barbara didn't realize how much it meant to her mother. She was happy to be on the *Hurricane*, but she didn't think it was that big a deal to be reunited with her family. She later remembered that Derek and Sonia were busy eating a big meal when they were reunited. But she didn't talk about her night on the ocean, not for years.

Only long after their mother died did Sonia and Derek find out that Barbara hadn't been worried. They thought she didn't talk about the event because it had been traumatic for her. In fact, she was one of the few who had not been traumatized that night.

....

THAT FIRST NIGHT on the *Hurricane* was uncomfortable for the Bechs and Colin. They had to sleep on the floor of a room, in sleeping bags, not beds. The ship was not steady and so the children kept sliding around.

The ship was not steady because the destroyer was dropping depth charges against possible U-boats in the area. Lieutenant Commander Simms was so furious about what had happened and all he had seen and heard—all those murdered children—that he was hell-bent on retaliation.

All night he dropped depth charges. Marguerite Bech was irritated. Forget about the Germans, she said. Let's just get home. Colin was thrown at one point and hit his head. The bump hurt, but it wasn't nearly as bad as what he'd been through on the lifeboat.

All night, the ship's doctor, Peter Collinson, took care of the very sick passengers. Most survived, but a few died, including at least one Indian sailor and, breaking the crew's heart, three of the children.

For all his ministrations, the doctor could not save the two boys with chicken pox: Alan Capel, Derek's younger brother, and Peter Short, Bill's younger brother. Terence Holmes, Ken Sparks's friend, also died in the night.

The next day, the crew buried the dead at sea. The sailors cried as Alan, Peter, and Terence were laid to rest in their watery grave, their little bodies wrapped in cloth.

LATER THAT DAY, Peter Collinson examined Bess. He had bandaged her ankle and put it in a splint. Her leg would be fine, but the doctor could see she wasn't recovering as well as her friend Beth. Why wasn't she cheery? She had made it through a harrowing twenty hours. On the *Hurricane* she had even met a sailor who knew her when she was three years old, a happy coincidence, a touch of home. Still she seemed so sad. The doctor knew, of course, what a hard ordeal she had been through. But was there something she was worrying about?

Take care of that young man, her father had told her. She hadn't. She didn't know whether she'd ever find out what happened to Louis. These thoughts kept going through her head over and over again.

Yes, Bess said Yes, I am worried about my little brother. He was only ten years old. Had he gotten on a lifeboat? Had he drowned? How would she tell her parents that she was coming home without Louis?

Two things had kept her alive as she held on to that keel. One was Beth; the other was the knowledge that she would have to get home and explain to her parents what happened to Louis. Now she was tortured. How could she tell them that her little brother had died, that they had lost their only son? What would she say?

The doctor tried to be reassuring. He said, What if I told you that some mummies and daddies will not be having anyone return? Your mummy and daddy will feel so much better than you think. So come on, cheer up.

But the thought of other children dying did not cheer her up. It would not cheer her parents, either. Her brother's absence weighed heavily as the ship sailed toward Scotland.

. . . .

WHAT *HAD* HAPPENED to Louis Walder?

Louis had been on lifeboat 11 with the beloved escort, Michael Rennie. Rennie had two of the littler children in his arms. Several other CORB children were on this boat, including Rex Thorne, who was thirteen and, like Louis, had a sister on the ship, Marion, Mary for short. Mary was younger, and Rex was very worried about her. There was a thirteen-year-old boy, George Crawford, and one of Mary Cornish's girls, Maureen Dixon, along with eleven others. Like so many of the lifeboats, it had tipped as it was being lowered, and Louis had fallen into the sea.

George Crawford saved Louis, pulling him back into the lifeboat. But then George lost his balance and fell into the ocean himself, and they never saw him again. That was just one of the tragedies on lifeboat 11.

Michael Rennie kept rescuing children. Michael dove in after them, one at a time, over and over again. Louis watched him with awe. Other adults on the boat warned Michael to stop, not to risk his own life, but Michael is reported to have replied, "There are still children in the water, and I must get them." He dove in for at least a dozen children.

It was a grueling night for Louis and Rex and everyone else in their boat. As the night wore on, most of the children Michael Rennie had pulled from the water died. Rex Thorne was terribly upset about his sister, fearing the worst. (And he was right. Mary Thorne was among the first to die, on Sybil Gilliat-Smith's lifeboat, along with Joyce Keeley and the Grimmond girls.) But Michael Rennie persuaded Rex and Louis and the others that help would be coming. He told them exactly what would happen and what they should do when the rescue ship arrived.

Louis listened and kept his hope up. Michael was his hero, and he said they would be rescued. As the new day dawned, they found a case of condensed milk. Everyone on the boat was given a tin, reported one of the crew later; this cheered them up for a bit. However, Michael Rennie got quieter and quieter. He was exhausted, wet, cold. His body was shutting down. He fell unconscious. Though help was close by, rescue at hand, Michael's body gave out, and he died before the *Hurricane* arrived. He was twenty-three years old. Louis was devastated.

Louis Walder and Rex Thorne were the only ones still alive out of the fifteen CORB children in their lifeboat. Both were in terrible shape. Rex couldn't stop shivering, even with a blanket wrapped around him. The bartender from the ship, Jimmy Proudfoot, held Rex in his arms. He kept an eye on Louis and prayed and prayed—the boys could not die like Michael Rennie, before rescue arrived.

....

NOW, ON THE *HURRICANE*, Johnny Baker kept looking for his brother. He ran everywhere and asked everyone. Once he said to one of the sailors, Excuse me, have you seen my brother, Bobby?

The sailor was none other than the captain of the ship, Lieutenant Commander Simms, and he looked at the seven-year-old and corrected him: Have you seen my brother, *sir*?

So Johnny replied, Have you seen my brother, sir? But the captain hadn't. Johnny Baker would never know exactly what happened to Bobby.

....

BESS WALDER LAY in bed, sick and sad. She heard Lieutenant Commander Simms banging on her door.

Sit up, miss! the captain yelled.

Bess sat up. You always did what the captain said, she reported later.

I have a present for you, little madam! Simms continued.

"And," Bess said decades later, reliving the joy of that moment, "from behind his back he produced my brother."

Taking a tour of the ship with some of the crew, Louis had seen a familiar green bathrobe, hanging in the boiler room, drying out.

That's my sister's! he told one of the sailors.

How do you know, son? the sailor asked him.

Because, Louis told him, that's the one she had a row with Mummy about before we left.

Now, looking at Louis, right there before her, Bess was overwhelmed with relief and joy. But her first instinct was to be angry.

WHERE HAVE YOU BEEN?! she yelled.

Well, what are *you* doing lying there?!

They hugged and kissed, but soon Louis was done with that, and so they just sat there together talking, happy and safe.

. . . .

BESS AND LOUIS were the only set of CORB siblings to survive. Johnny Baker lost his brother, Bobby. Jack Keeley lost his sister, Joyce. Rex Thorne lost his sister. All the Grimmond children died. The pairs of sisters in Mary's group died.

And on and on.

"Just how fortunate we were hadn't really dawned on us," Bess said years later, remembering. "The wreckage of lives also meant the wreckage of mothers' and fathers' lives too when they heard."

CHAPTER 20

....

"In Spite of All the Precautions"

AS THE *HURRICANE* made its way to the port of Greenock, not far from Glasgow, Scotland, CORB officials and the Ellerman City Line were making lists of people who had died and people who had lived. Geoffrey Shakespeare, head of the CORB program, was preparing a letter to the parents.

On the ship, the survivors began to recover from their ordeal. Sonia Bech found a small cat, black and white. It kept her company as she thought of home again. Mackie, her dog, would be there waiting for her. So would Derek's tabby cat, Tim. The Bechs were extremely fortunate to have one another, like Bess and Louis. But for so many, for most, the loss was unfathomable.

The survivors—crew, passengers, the remaining escorts—began to take in the immensity of the tragedy. At this point it seemed—though this turned out to be wrong—only seven out of the ninety CORB children survived. More than half of the escorts had died, too.

Of the children who were traveling privately on the ship with their families—or alone, as Colin Ryder Richardson was—six out of ten survived.

Husbands lost wives, wives lost husbands. Children lost parents. Whole families died. Almost half the British crew died, and more than half of the Indian crew.

Back in England, parents would soon learn their children had died, children they had sent away to be safe.

Geoffrey Shakespeare wrote a draft of the form letter that would be personalized and sent to the parents of the eighty-three children presumed dead:

Three of the surviving children:
(from left to right) Sonia Bech, Colin Ryder Richardson,
and Derek Bech. [Mary Evans Picture Library]

I am very distressed to inform you
that in spite of all the precautions taken
the ship carrying your child to Canada
was torpedoed on Tuesday night, September
17th. I am afraid your child was not
among those reported as rescued, and I am
informed that there is no chance of there
being any further lists of survivors from
the torpedoed vessel.

The Children's Overseas Reception Board
wishes me to convey its very deep sympathy
with you in your bereavement. Like so
many other parents you were anxious to
send your child overseas to one of the
Dominions to enjoy a happier and safer
life. You courageously took this decision
in the interest of your child, believing
that this course was better than leaving
the child here in a vulnerable area
subject to continuous air raids. Hitherto
there have been no casualties among the
thousands of children sent overseas.
Unhappily the course of the war has shown
that neither by land nor sea can there be
complete safety and all of us are subject
to the risk whether we stay at home or
proceed overseas.

As a parent I can realise the anguish
that this letter must cause you and the
great sadness which will be brought into
your home. I should like to assure you how
profoundly I, personally, sympathise with
you and how deeply I share your grief.

Yours very truly,
Geoffrey Shakespeare

THE LETTERS ARRIVED at parents' homes on Friday, September 20, a week after the ship had sailed, a little over a week after the children had left home. Johnny Baker's mother told a reporter from the *Daily Mirror* that her sons had been looking forward to a grand time in Canada: "We were expecting a cablegram to tell us that they had arrived safely when the education officer came to say their ship had been torpedoed. We are so thankful that we still have Johnny."

Eddie and Hannah Grimmond received the letters from Gussie and Violet and Connie on the same day they got the official letter. "Please do not answer this letter," Gussie had written, "as I will be in mid-Atlantic."

The families of the escorts received letters, too. Michael Rennie's parents were devastated. Michael was a shining light, now gone. His father, the vicar, would write to Louis Walder and ask him for details about his son, which Louis would give him. And later, the

Johnny Baker (left) and Rex Thorne after their rescue. [Shutterstock]

CHILDREN'S OVERSEAS RECEPTION BOARD
45, BERKELEY STREET
LONDON
W.I

Replies to this communication should be
addressed to the Director-General,
quoting S.5791.

Telephone : Mayfair 8400.
Telegrams : Avoncorb, London.

Your reference...........................

22nd September, 1940.

Dear Mr. Paterson,

       I am deeply distressed to inform you that in
spite of all the precautions taken, the ship on which
your sister-in-law, Miss Mary Cornish, was accompanying
children to Canada was torpedoed on Tuesday night,
September 17th.   I have to tell you that your sister-
in-law was not among those reported as rescued and am
afraid that there is no chance of there being any
further lists of survivors from the torpedoed vessel.

       The Children's Overseas Reception Board wishes
me to convey to you its very deep sympathy in your grievous
loss.   Your sister-in-law courageously undertook the duty
of acting as escort to these children as a contribution to
national service.   She lost her life in the protection of
the children, and on behalf of the Board and of the parents
I should like to express to you our appreciation of this
gallant devotion to duty.

       Yours sincerely,

       Geoffrey Shakespeare.

Ian Paterson, Esq.,
Bywood,
West Lavington,
Midhurst, Sussex.

vicar had a mural painted in his church depicting Michael's heroism as described by Louis and others on the boat. Louis and Bess visited the vicar, and he asked Louis to sit for the mural, which he did.

Mary Cornish's younger sister, Eileen Paterson, was bereft. Their mother had died when Eileen was very young. When their father remarried, Eileen took it very hard. From that time on, she had depended on Mary. Mary gave her the love and support she needed. Eileen was married, with two small children, and she had been distraught when Mary went off as a CORB escort. She couldn't wait for her sister to come back and be close by again. Mary wasn't just a beloved teacher and a devoted aunt; she was, to Eileen, an irreplaceable sister.

But now she received a letter with the worst news. On September 22, Geoffrey Shakespeare wrote a letter to Eileen's husband, Ian Paterson.

In those first days after they received the news, the parents and families of the dead children and the escorts, of all the passengers who did not survive, were shattered. They did what they could, planned and held memorial services, all the while in shock and grief.

But in the case of six of the CORB families, the letters from CORB were incorrect—either completely or partially. For there was one lifeboat from the *Benares* that had not been seen by the *Hurricane*. That lifeboat was still at sea, and it was packed with forty-six passengers. Among them were six CORB boys and two escorts. It was Mary Cornish's lifeboat, number 12.

The story of the torpedoing of the SS *City of Benares* should have been over, but it was not.

Opposite: *This letter from Geoffrey Shakespeare to Mary Cornish's brother-in-law was, it would turn out, incorrect.*
[Courtesy of Maggie Paterson, photograph by author]

....

CHAPTER 21

Lifeboat 12

RONNIE COOPER, THE *City of Benares*'s fourth officer, was in command of lifeboat 12. He was twenty-two years old. He'd been asleep when the torpedo hit and had been awakened by a dull explosion. He dressed in a hurry, and when he heard the alarm gongs, rushed to his station, lifeboat 12. The eighteen lascar crew members assigned to his boat were already mustered.

Six CORB boys—Fred Steels, Paul Shearing, Ken Sparks, Howard Claytor, Bill Short, and Derek Capel—were already in the boat, as was Father Rory O'Sullivan. Mary Cornish had made the decision to get in it, too.

Before lowering the lifeboat, Cooper had sent the assistant steward, George Purvis, twenty-three, to make sure there were no children asleep or trapped in cabins. And then he held the lifeboat in place. He did not lower it for fifteen minutes—"in case any stragglers happened to appear." He wanted to save as many people as he could.

The boat swayed on its ropes, the storm's rain and wind adding to its instability. But he wanted to make sure. Finally Cooper decided it was time. He ordered the four lascars who had been waiting to lower it, and as it went down, Mary Cornish felt a violent jerk. But this was one of the few lifeboats that lowered straight onto the water, without a hitch. Nobody fell out, no water was taken into the boat. The six boys were safe.

Safe but scared. And worried. Especially the two boys who had brothers on the ship: Derek Capel and Bill Short. Hearing the screams of children plummeting into the water was horrible. Derek was terribly worried about Alan. Was one of those children his brother?

Just five days earlier, he had held his little brother's hand as they stood in line with their group to board the *City of Benares*. Now he had no idea where Alan was. Although his memory would change over the years, and he'd think Alan had been with him when the torpedo hit, others remembered that Alan had been in the infirmary with chicken pox. Getting into lifeboat 12, Father Rory had tried to reassure him that Alan must have gotten in another lifeboat.

The Capels hadn't wanted to send their sons away. But Mr. Capel had Jewish relatives. And with Hitler's anti-Jewish rhetoric, they knew that if the Nazis took over England, Jewish people would be in even more danger. So after a great deal of heart-searching, they applied for CORB. At five years old, Alan was as young as a CORB child could be.

Bill Short was nine and the youngest boy on lifeboat 12. His little brother, Peter, also five, had been in the infirmary with chicken pox, too.

Even for those who didn't have brothers to worry about, the screams were horrifying. For Fred Steels, the most traumatic part was hearing the other children screaming and not being able to do anything about it.

With the boat bobbing on the water, the lascars climbed down the ropes into it. So did George Purvis, who would be a tremendous help to Cooper. Cooper himself was still on the deck of the *Benares*. He took one more look around to make sure there were no children, and nobody else who needed rescuing, and then climbed down into the lifeboat himself.

Just as they were getting clear of the ship, Cooper noticed four more lascars scrambling down the lifelines. He ordered the lifeboat put back near the ship to take them in. Then they maneuvered away.

....

AFTER THE SHIP SANK, Cooper plucked people out of the water, including six more lascars and sea cadet Doug Critchley. In addition to Doug, the boat now had Royal Navy men Johnny Mayhew and gunner Harry Peard. All three would prove very useful.

Cooper saw a light. He thought it was a rescue ship, so he steered right for it. When he got closer, he saw it was another lifeboat, but not one from the *Benares*. The passengers greeted him.

What ship are you from? they asked.

The *Benares*, he responded.

We are from the *Marina*, they told him.

Upon hearing that, Cooper decided to keep company with them. The two boats steered in an easterly direction using the strong wind and keeping the swelling sea to their stern.

The people on lifeboat 12 spent much the same kind of night as the survivors on the other lifeboats, with two big exceptions: there were a lot of them, and all the children lived through the night, as cold and lightly dressed as most of them were. The lascars were in such thin clothes, too. But with so many people in the boat, the body heat in the cramped quarters kept them warmer than they would have been otherwise.

Kenneth Sparks was warm; he was wearing a coat. He had gone back to his cabin to get it, and that was how he ended up on this particular lifeboat.

Ken, at thirteen, was the oldest of the CORB boys on lifeboat 12. He lived in Wembley, in outer London, with his father, stepmother, and three-year-old sister. Ken was supposed to be on his way to his stepmother's relatives in Edmonton, Alberta. Before this trip, the war hadn't affected his life much. The biggest change was less school, because some schools were closed and the ones that stayed open had to share buildings. His school hours had been cut in half. That happened during the Phony War, which was what they called the time before the war actually hit England. Lately, though, with the air raids and bombings, he'd felt the war more. He'd managed to collect some shrapnel, and his parents had taken him to see the London Docklands fire just the week before he started on this trip.

Now he was right *in* the war, wasn't he?

Ken didn't know what had happened to his friend Terence Holmes. Terry lived up the road, and they played together all the time. Ken and Terry and the other boys on the ship had had so much fun. Watching the crew at work, looking at the other ships in the convoy. And the food. How Ken had loved the meals. So terrific compared with what he'd been having at home, where the meals were modest. He especially loved the desserts. So many, as many as he liked! It had been a long way up to the dining room, Ken remembered, all those stairs, but it was worth it.

After the torpedo struck, it had all happened so fast. Like so many others, Ken owed his life to luck—but in his case, fear of his stepmother had also helped.

Ken had been sound asleep. But a loud noise woke him up. Then the lights flickered on and off, and he heard yelling. He made sure the three younger boys in his cabin got out and into the corridor. Nobody was panicking; everyone was walking, not running, walking quite calmly toward the main staircase.

Out in the hall, Ken realized he didn't have his overcoat, so he ducked out of line and headed back to his cabin. He didn't want to upset his mum—he didn't think of her as a stepmother, just as a mother—though he did wonder whether she'd been eager for him to go abroad so she could bring in some money by renting out his room. Still, he worried she would be mad if he didn't come home with that nice overcoat.

My mum'll kill me, he thought. So he went back and got it.

When he got back into the queue, his young roommates were farther along. He stayed in the back. His roommates made their way up the main staircase, through the dining room, and onto the deck. So did he. The wind was blowing, and it was raining like mad. He had to walk around a great big hole to get to his station. The crew guided him, and as he was walking toward his lifeboat, which was supposed to be number 8, a sailor picked him up, a man whose name he never knew, and said, There's room in this boat, son, and he just put him in. That was lifeboat 12. And here he was, with the other boys and Auntie Mary.

Mary Cornish had no time to change, so she had on the same clothes she'd been wearing during her stroll on the deck with her friends: a thin silk blouse, a thin skirt, a short-sleeved jacket, silk stockings, and sandals. The bitter, damp cold went through her until she was numb.

She also was wretchedly seasick from the choppy waters, the boat going up and down, up and down, rocking on the waves. She had hurt herself breaking through the debris and pulling children out, but between the nausea and the cold, she didn't yet feel the pain from her shredded skin and bruises—that would come later.

....

WHEN DAWN CAME, Ronnie Cooper saw the *Marina*'s lifeboat set sail. He did not follow. He felt that the weather was too heavy for his boat to sail in, so they just carried on rowing with the Fleming gear.

Cooper's decision not to sail was a sound and practical one, but it left the tiny craft alone in the vast Atlantic. It would be missed by the rescue ship.

The good news was that the boat was steady, in part because it was so full of people. That was also the bad news: it was a very crowded. Could they be comfortable? And more important—crucial, in fact—would there be enough food and water for everyone to last however long it took to be rescued, or to reach land? Fortunately, Cooper was aware that they might not be rescued soon and began to make plans.

There were thirty-two lascars, including a man named Ramjam Buxoo, who had been exceptionally steady and calm the night before, helping people into lifeboats. There was also the assistant steward, George Purvis, and the three sailors they'd picked up: Doug Critchley, Johnny Mayhew, and Harry Peard. Only one paying passenger from the ship had made it into lifeboat 12, a man from Poland, Bohdan Nagorski, the man who had been walking on deck when Mary was with her friends. He was the managing director of a steamship company. (Nagorski's friend, the diplomat, did not survive.)

Nagorski had escaped from the Germans twice so far—once in Poland and then in German occupied France. Now he was trying again to stay alive. He was one of the lifeboat's few well-dressed people—wearing a fur coat over clothes, a felt hat on his head.

....

COOPER REARRANGED THE people in the boat, putting the children, the two escorts, and Nagorski in the bow. To allow more room, he had the handles removed from the rowing equipment there. But the sockets remained, and the passengers had to maneuver around them. The adults wrapped the boys in blankets that had been found in the night. Cooper also had the crew rig a canvas tarp over the bow. It would help protect the boys from the weather. The tarp was so low that the adults had to lie down under it or sit on the floor of the boat. Father Rory O'Sullivan was lying down anyway. He was sick, and kept vomiting. He might not live long.

In the stern were Cooper, Purvis, Critchley, Mayhew, and Peard, though Peard moved around a lot, talking with everyone. The Indian crewmen sat in the middle. Most of them didn't speak much English, but Ramjam Buxoo was able to communicate with both the British crew and his fellow lascars.

On that first day, Cooper put all the occupants of the boat on food and water rations just in case they weren't rescued. He had asked George Purvis to assess how much food and water they had, and instructed him to plan ahead. Purvis knew that meant to plan for the worst-case scenario: sailing this boat to Ireland. That would take more than a week, at best. Purvis would have to be detailed, methodical, and conservative about it, rationing the food and water so that each person would have enough. It would be a challenge.

Purvis looked in the metal lockers and found cans of salmon, sardines, corned beef, peaches and pineapple, and tins of sweetened condensed milk. And there were ship's biscuits, hard as stone and good only if you had water to wash them down. There was a good amount of fresh water in the boat's jug, but was it enough? Purvis and Cooper knew the water would be the biggest problem. Although there was more water per person than was regulation, Purvis calculated there would not be enough for the forty-six on board if they had to sail to Ireland. He had to figure out how to make it last. The food, too, but the water most of all. After a few days nobody would be hungry, but thirst would only get worse. A person can live without food for weeks. But you can't go more than a few days without water.

Purvis served the first meal at noon on Wednesday, the day after the torpedo hit, the day the other survivors would be rescued. Purvis opened the bag of ship's biscuits and the sardines. He made a kind of open-faced sandwich for each person: a ship's biscuit with a sardine on top. One at a time, a biscuit with sardine was passed from person to person—first to the children and Mary Cornish and Rory O'Sullivan, then to the lascars, and last to the crew and Nagorski.

When everyone had a biscuit and sardine, it was time for water. The lifeboat had on board a thin cylindrical beaker made just for this purpose. Purvis filled the beaker, and then it, too, was passed—carefully—to the first person, who drank it and passed it back to Purvis, who would refill it and send it out again to the next person.

The boys ate their biscuit and sardine, and drank their water. They talked about the torpedo and what had happened. But like all the other survivors from the *Benares* that day, mostly they looked at the horizon for a ship coming to rescue them.

The doling out of lunch took over an hour. It required cooperation, good nature, and a sense of community. Each person had to wait his turn, and had to resist the temptation to take someone else's ration.

Just as the U-boat was a contained community bound by fate, a small vessel that needed harmony to function well and avert danger, so too was a lifeboat. Trust in the leader—Cooper—was crucial. Keeping peace was vital for survival, too. They had to develop systems whereby nobody got angry and everyone helped.

The adults took turns rowing. Although he was ill, Father Rory took up the oars when it was his turn. But he was so weak from days of vomiting and not eating that he passed out.

When he came to, he was wrapped in someone's jacket. He heard people saying they didn't think the father would last much longer.

....

AT SOME POINT during the day, Mary took off her petticoat so that lifeboat 12 would have something to run up the mast as a flag if a plane or a ship came near.

As the first day ended with no rescue ship in sight, Cooper and Purvis doled out the second meal: a can of sweetened condensed milk for everyone, another ship's biscuit, and some water. Again it took an hour. It was good to take up time because there was so much of it.

The sky grew dark. It seemed a certainty to them that there would not, indeed, be rescue on this day.

The passengers on lifeboat 12 settled down to sleep—except those who were steering the boat or keeping watch. Under the tarp, the boys and Mary and sick Father Rory got as comfortable as they could, which was not at all comfortable. There were the sockets from the Fleming gear, and a locker—the space was so cramped that if someone moved an arm or a leg, the person next to him had to move a limb, too. And it was so very cold. There were not enough blankets for everyone.

The weather did not cooperate; a storm was raging again. The wind blew so fiercely that Father Rory worried the boat would capsize in the night.

CHAPTER 22

··

I Spy Nothing

DAWN CAME. FATHER Rory O'Sullivan was still terribly sick, but he rallied enough to lead the boys in the Lord's Prayer. "Our Father, who art in heaven, hallowed be thy name; thy kingdom come; thy will be done, on earth as it is in heaven."

The lascars also prayed first thing in the morning, and would pray four other times during the day. They washed themselves with seawater as best they could, before chanting the prayer. Just like Father Rory, they were praising God.

With prayers and hope, and good planning, the passengers of lifeboat 12 had a chance to survive. Mary Cornish looked at the six boys and knew she had the most important task of her life—to keep these children alive.

A big problem would be boredom. Bill, Derek, Ken, Fred, Paul, and Howard were used to running around. On the ship they had followed the crew everywhere, watching them work, asking them questions, and had stood at the rails waving to the other ships in the convoy.

And back home, before they'd left, they'd had the run of their neighborhoods, as all British kids did back then, playing freely in their yards or even the streets. On days without school, children would be out all day, with an apple and some cookies in their pockets, running about, riding bicycles if they had them, even on major roads. They'd bring a cricket bat and a ball and play wherever they could, against stumps or stoops, using coats as wickets. They'd play running and chasing games, like tag, touch, poison, crusts and crumbs, blind man's buff, and leapfrog. They'd play with marbles and climb trees.

When the war came to England, the buildings leveled by bombs became ruins to explore. Children would climb onto piles of rubble and look for treasure: pieces of toys, broken clocks, furniture, dishes, and shrapnel, sometimes even a piece of a German air plane.

And they had watched the planes. Many of these boys had front-row seats to the dogfights in the sky. They'd gotten to know not just the looks but also the sounds of the different British planes versus the German planes. They could identify a Spitfire, a Hurricane, a German Dornier, a Messerschmitt, a Heinkel.

On rainy days, of course, children would have books and toys and games to occupy them. They'd build with their metal Meccano sets, play card and board games, checkers. They'd listen to the radio, to war reports on the BBC Home Service, and on Saturdays, no matter the weather, there was the tuppenny rush for a movie and the newsreels.

On lifeboat 12 there was no radio, no cards or board games, no books to read, or films to watch. Worst of all, there was nowhere to *go*. They could barely move, the boat was so cramped.

Some of the boys were still seasick, the boat rocking on the high waves, up and down, their stomachs churning. Mary Cornish tried to think how to keep them diverted from their fear, their boredom, their seasickness, their cold. And for Bill Short and Derek Capel, from their worries about their little brothers.

First they sang. Mary was a music teacher after all. They sang "There'll Always Be an England," just as they had when the *City of Benares* set sail, and "Roll Out the Barrel" and "Run, Rabbit, Run," as well as the popular parody version of that tune:

> Run rabbit, run rabbit, run, run, run.
> Run rabbit, run rabbit, run, run, run.
> Bang, bang, bang, bang goes the farmer's gun.
> Run rabbit, run rabbit, run, run, run, run.
> Run rabbit, run rabbit, run, run, run.
> Don't give the farmer his fun, fun, fun.
> He'll get by without his rabbit pie.
> So run rabbit, run rabbit, run, run, run.
> Run Adolf, run Adolf, run, run, run.
> Now that the fun has begun, gun, gun.

....

AND THERE STILL was, of course, a lot of talk about what had happened. They hashed it out over and over again. They had been torpedoed! (It was only a torpedo . . .) They talked about where they had been: in bed! They'd had a bath. They were in their pajamas for the first time. When the torpedo hit, they were asleep.

What they heard: loud noise, alarm bells, ringing like the dickens.

What happened: top bunk fell on top of Fred! He got soaking wet! Lights flickering, confusion . . .

Ken got his coat . . .

The smell of cordite!

How they got to the lifeboat: breaking through walls, finding Father Rory, Father Rory finding them. Confusion . . .

Where was this friend? and that one?

And the brothers, the little brothers?

And there was this question over and over: Would you rather be torpedoed at sea or bombed at home?

The bombs at home were scary. They destroyed houses and schools and churches, and they killed people. They all knew that. Fred had had a couple of close calls. So many air raids. He had survived not only the air raids but also his landlady, Mrs. Stellard, sitting on top of him. Whenever the air raid siren sounded, she would throw Fred under the stairs and sit on him to protect him.

One night Fred and his parents and the landlady heard a loud banging on the door. It was Mr. Wilding, the air raid warden.

Quick, he said, you have to get out. There's a bomb right next door!

A bomb had landed on the roof, skidded across it, and gone inside the neighbor's house—must have been through a window—down the front stairs and had landed at the front door. It was ticking.

Ticking . . .

Fred and his family ran out of their house and away from the neighbor's.

But the bomb didn't go off. Fred was safe.

And now he was in the middle of the Atlantic Ocean. Bombed at home or torpedoed at sea? He chose torpedoed at sea. All the boys did. This was an adventure! So far.

. . . .

BUT AFTER ALL the talk, the rehashing, the *would you rather*s, boredom set in quickly. Their one built-in diversion was when they had to go to the bathroom. There was no bathroom. There was just a bucket to urinate in, or do the other, when necessary. So when they had to go, they asked for the bucket and tried their best to do their business in it. The contents were then dumped in the sea. When it was Mary's turn, everybody looked the other way.

After a few days, there would be little need for the bucket. They would be eating so little, and drinking even less, that their bodies would not have much of anything to get rid of.

Anyway, the bucket was already not enough entertainment. Mary tried playing games. Animal, vegetable, mineral. One of the boys would say, "I'm thinking of . . ." And the others would ask questions to discover what he had in mind. It worked for a while, and then they got tired of it.

They played "I spy." What did they spy?

Each other.

The other people on the boat.

Parts of the boat: sail, mast, tiller, handles, a jug of drinking water, tins of bully beef (canned corned beef). At sea there was—the sea. Waves, clouds, spray. A very few seabirds.

The bathroom bucket.

But there was not much to spy that nobody else could. It was too easy to guess.

There was a surplus of what they could *not* spy:

- other lifeboats from the *Benares*
- lifeboats from any other ship
- fishing boats
- cruise ships
- oilers
- destroyers
- sailboats
- yachts
- rescuers
- land

- Mum
- Dad
- little brothers
- all the people who weren't in lifeboat 12

There was so little to see and so much to long for. "I spy," it turned out, was no fun, no fun at all.

Mary had to think of something.

So she began telling a story.

She made Bulldog Drummond the hero. Created by author Cyril McNeile in 1920, Bulldog Drummond was the protagonist in a popular series of novels and movies. Mary started with what she remembered and made up the rest.

Captain Hugh Drummond was a handsome bloke, over six feet tall with a square jaw and a crooked nose, injured in the boxing ring when he was a teenager. He had a lot of money and too much time on his hands. Drummond was home from the First World War, and he was bored. He put an advertisement in the paper: "Demobilised officer, finding peace incredibly tedious, would welcome diversion. Legitimate, if possible; but crime, if of a comparatively humorous description, no objection. Excitement essential."

Captain Drummond got mixed up in solving crimes, in a rather bumbling sort of way, usually with his life very much in danger. He had a nemesis, and a fiancée. Hugh Drummond was stubborn and determined, and he would get a certain look on his face, which earned him the nickname Bulldog.

Bulldog never underestimated his opponent, neither in the boxing ring nor in the war. And, he declared, "he had no intention of doing so" when he was fighting bad guys.

He was the perfect scrappy hero for children far away from home, in a lifeboat in the middle of the ocean in the middle of a war. Mary had

Bulldog Drummond get deeply embroiled with a gang of Nazi spies. He fought them in planes, submarines, parachutes. He used secret radio installations, masterminds, and codes. The Nazis fought back; he got in serious danger. When Mary couldn't think of a way out for her hero, she stopped.

NO! the boys cried. Don't stop!

That's it for now, Mary told them.

Go on, Auntie. Please go on! they pleaded.

She promised the boys more soon. This gave them something to look forward to, something to wait for, and it gave her time to make up more of the story, she hoped.

In the next few hours, she remembered bits from *The Thirty-Nine Steps*, a novel written in 1915 and made into a movie by Alfred Hitchcock in 1935, just five years earlier. *The Thirty-Nine Steps* also had a hero, an upper-crust Englishman, Richard Hannay, who got entangled with spies and murderers. Mary used what she remembered from Hannay's exploits, too.

And so began a routine. Prayers in the morning led by Father Rory, and stories from Mary. She'd give them an installment after the midday meal and then another one before they settled down for the night after some sweetened condensed milk.

Would Mary have enough in her to keep telling the stories as long as they were at sea? That was a mystery she had no answer to. She had no idea how long it would be before they were rescued. Or, not rescued.

But she was determined to keep those boys alive by telling them such a suspenseful story that they couldn't wait to hear more.

Mary Cornish was a hero in her own story, and like any good hero, she had obstacles to overcome: the open sea, the threat of more storms, the cold and wind, the lack of water. Like any hero, she had adversaries.

CHAPTER 23

Perils at Sea

MARY CORNISH'S FIERCEST adversary was time. The boys had boarded lifeboat 12 well-fed and healthy, thanks to the abundance of delicious food on the ship. Their extra stores of fat, even from those few days on the ship, would help keep them alive longer. But this extra fat would be depleted as every day went by, especially since the food portions on the lifeboat had to be very small. More than food, they needed water. There would not be enough if they weren't rescued soon. Purvis and Cooper knew that. Purvis would do his best to stretch it out as long as he could.

Against them also were other stresses: the extreme cold, fear, boredom, and damage to their bodies because they couldn't move around much. The human body is fragile when placed under dire stress. If they weren't rescued soon enough, the boys' organs would start to shut down. They were just boys, after all. Bill was nine; Fred, Paul, and Howard were eleven; Derek was twelve; and Ken, thirteen. They were only human.

So was Mary.

In her very thin clothes, she already was feeling the effects from exposure, intense cold, and exhaustion. She hurt from her bruises and cuts. And she was suffering from lack of water. She felt the mental and emotional stress of keeping the boys alive singlehandedly—Father Rory was so sick and weak. But the huge responsibility gave her a reason to stay strong, to stay alive.

Her strength was tested every now and again by a human adversary: the most outspoken, active, and vibrant man on the boat, Harry Peard.

Peard was one of the navy gunners on the *City of Benares*. At thirty-eight years old, he had been the oldest gunner on the ship, and now on lifeboat 12, he was much older than Ronnie Cooper, the captain of the lifeboat, and George Purvis, the steward in charge of the food and water. Peard was small and wiry—five feet four inches tall, athletic and agile. He could easily get around the boat, stepping over, or on, whoever was in his way. He got along well with the lascars. Even though he didn't speak their language, he had a way of communicating with them. He was cheerful and funny and made everyone laugh.

When it came to how things should be done on the lifeboat, Peard was quite opinionated and not afraid to speak his mind, whether it was to Cooper or Purvis, one of the Indian crew, or even Mary Cornish.

In many ways, Peard was a real-life hero, a true role model for the boys, right there in their very close quarters. He told them that when the torpedo hit, he had been in the gunner's nest on lookout and had been thrown directly into the ocean by the force of the impact. Others later reported that he rescued children who had fallen into the water, swimming them to lifeboats.

Peard wasn't an upper-crust hero like Bulldog Drummond or Richard Hannay. He was rough, full of energy and salty language. And he could be a show-off. When the weather was decent—when it wasn't storming—he'd strip down to his trunks and dive into the water. He'd swim around the boat two or three times. Sometimes he would even pretend to be drowning to make the boys laugh.

One time one of the boys asked him, Why are you swimming, mister?

And he answered, Why, to keep in practice in case we get torpedoed again! The boys erupted in laughter. The idea of a U-boat torpedoing a little lifeboat was too funny.

He's a proper screwball, thought Fred. But one of the nicest chaps you could meet. He and the other boys were glad to have him on board.

But he could really get in Mary's way. She was grateful whenever he cheered up her boys, but when he didn't agree with something she was doing, he was harsh and could easily undo the good she'd done.

He seemed to have a knack for showing up in her part of the boat at just the wrong moment—when one of the boys had kicked his legs clear of his bit of blanket or when another had just woken up to complain of the cold.

Here, what's all this? he'd yell. This boy doesn't have a blanket! No wonder he's cold, poor little guy. Come on, son, let's tuck the blanket under—that's the way. Ought to be someone keeping an eye on these kids.

Of course that's just what Mary *was* doing. A few times he was personally nasty to her, saying that his wife could have done better because she had children of her own. Mary had no children, he pointed out—and wasn't likely to either, he added.

You're right on both counts, Mary responded. And what of it?

He was tough on Rory O'Sullivan, too. He told the priest to stop lying about and praying so much.

Mary stood up for Rory, explaining that he was sick, which of course Peard knew.

But in truth Peard did respect Mary, especially her storytelling. When Mary's voice started to give out, Peard came to their part of the boat and taught the boys salty old songs, maybe changing some of the dirty words, maybe not. He taught them "My Old Man Said Follow the Van" and "Any Old Iron":

> Any old iron, any old iron,
> any, any, old, old iron?
> You look neat, talk about a treat,
> you look dapper from your napper to your feet.
> Dress'd in style, brand new tile,
> and your father's old green tie on,
> but I wouldn't give you tuppence for your old
>   watch chain,
> old iron, old iron?

Bohdan Nagorski thought Peard was terrific, keeping up the spirits of everyone on the boat, especially the lascars. Peard was always ready for any difficult job in the boat, Nagorski noticed with admiration.

But Mary was furious when she heard him say—within earshot of the boys—that it was likely they wouldn't reach Ireland alive.

When that was all she was trying to do.

Keep those boys alive.

....

THE WEATHER WAS good their fourth day at sea, so Cooper had the sail up and they were going at a good clip. Doug Critchley, the twenty-year-old cadet, was proving to be a great asset to the boat. Father Rory was quite impressed. Critchley lived in Liverpool and was an avid sailor back home. Here, on the lifeboat, Father Rory admired his expertise at the tiller. Critchley also did more than his share of the watches. He asked Father Rory if he would teach him French. The priest said he would, if he felt better, but he never did.

For a while on this day with the nice weather, Father Rory was well enough to stand up and take a look around. Scanning the vast ocean, he noticed a pod of whales.

It was something to see, finally, for the boys. Whales! Everyone look! What a great spectacle. Soon the whales seemed to surround the boat.

The boys loved it. The whales were so huge and so close, their big tails flapping on the water as they dove under. And then the great surprise of where they'd come back up again! Maybe on the other side of the boat, maybe—

And then the crew realized that if the whales got too close or came up under the boat, they could smash it all to pieces. So lifeboat 12 was steered away from that potential danger.

There were many perils at sea. The trick was to outsmart them.

CHAPTER 24

....

British Heroes
Don't Snivel

DAY FIVE. STILL nothing in sight: no boats, no planes, no sign of rescue.

The boys were not doing well. Their bodies were wasting away. Their feet were terribly sore, from the cold and wet and poor blood circulation. They weren't moving around much.

Mary remembered back to her other life, before all this. She had rubbed the hands of her piano students before recitals. So she began rubbing the boys' hands and feet to keep the circulation going. She did this, all day and through the night if they were sleepless. She herself hardly slept. She had to stay awake to keep the boys alive. Her friends in England, who thought she was dead, would not be at all surprised by her devotion to the boys.

Mary stuck to the routine: a story after the midday meal and before bed. It was an uphill battle. She could barely talk. Or think. Yet she kept up with the Bulldog Drummond story as best she could. The anticipation kept the boys going.

Throughout the boat, the days at sea, the lack of water and food, and the cold were taking their toll. The Indian men were failing. Some seemed to be going in and out of consciousness; others were delirious.

Everyone was upset, scared, depressed, and sometimes cranky.

And thirsty. The boys were told to suck on their buttons. Ken Sparks sucked on a little lamb—a religious token that Father Rory had given him back on the ship.

Sometimes, when they had a spurt of energy, the boys would talk again about what happened. And they would ask, Would you rather be torpedoed at sea or bombed at home? The answer now, resoundingly, for all of them, was bombed at home.

They wanted to be home.

They longed for home.

And they worried about their pocket money. It was gone, down with the ship. What would they do? What would their parents say if they came back without their money? Bohdan Nagorski told them that when they were rescued and landed back home, he would give them the pocket money they'd lost. *When* they were rescued, not if. They'd have their money back. Here was another hero, right there on the boat.

Sometimes the boys talked about how thirsty they were. It was unbearable, truly. Their mouths were so dry, their lips parched and cracked. Their tongues sore and swollen.

They weren't as hungry, though at times they craved food. They liked thinking of it, dreaming of it, imagining what they would eat if they could, just like Richard Hannay, the hero of *The Thirty-Nine Steps*.

Hannay is on the lam, running away from the police, who are after him for a murder he did not commit. He's hiding from the real murderers, tucked into the moors of Scotland, with only crumbles of ginger cookies in his pocket, dreaming of all the food he should have enjoyed more in London: "crisp sausages and fragrant shavings of bacon, shapely poached eggs," ham that stood on the cold table at his club, for which he now lusted. He finally settles on what he would eat if he could: "a porter-house steak and a quart of bitter with a Welsh rabbit to follow."

The food on the ship, just days ago, was so delicious and plentiful, as the food must be in a first-class hotel, thought Fred Steels. Now the ship's biscuits had become too hard for the boys to eat without enough water to wash them down. They were so hard you could break a tooth on them, it seemed to Fred. Sometimes the only way sailors could eat hardtack was to leave it until it got stale and soft, but by then the biscuits would be crawling with weevils and maggots. None of the boys wanted the biscuits anymore anyway, but they couldn't very well throw them overboard, so they gave them to Auntie Mary to hold, just in case they might want them later. Mary's pockets were full of ship's biscuits.

The boys ate the little bit of bully beef or the sardines and the cold, sweet peach slices, but they dreamed of real food. Full meals. What they would eat when they were rescued.

Just like Richard Hannay, they fantasized: roast beef and Yorkshire pudding, of course, *the* thing for a mouth-watering Sunday dinner. They dreamed of sausages for breakfast, and jelly roll for dessert. Sometimes they wanted just the usual, like fish-and-chips.

But what about when they were rescued or reached land? If they made it to Ireland, they would eat Irish stew. If they landed in Scotland, they would have Scottish broth. For a few moments they wondered, If they got to Scotland, would they get kilts?

And what would they drink? For some reason sarsaparilla was the thing. Everyone wanted a sarsaparilla, even the boys who had never tasted it.

TIME STARTED TO BLUR. Their world got smaller and smaller. Everything was the cramped boat, the sliver of sardine, a sweet slice of peach, Bulldog Drummond, each other, Auntie Mary. Longing for home. They got sad.

Why were they here? It was like they had gone from a palace to a dungeon, not because they were bad, but because they were lucky. Where was Derek's little bother? Bill's? Would Ken ever get back to his little sister? Or Fred to his parents, who had lost so many? Howard was an only child. What if—

Give us more stories, Auntie, they pleaded, but Mary's lips were so swollen, her tongue encrusted with salt. And with her brain on so little sleep, could she?

She did. Fortitude was the only way through.

And with the boys heavyhearted, weary, yearning for home, Mary brought out some stiff upper lip: British heroes don't snivel, she told them.

We are British.

We will be rescued.

But the boys were so achy and tired and cold and weak and thirsty and—

British heroes don't snivel, Mary said.

Be brave.

They tried. They were.

And then . . .

The passengers on lifeboat 12 saw something.

Could it be a ship? A destroyer? Come to rescue them?

....

CHAPTER 25

Hope Is a Fine Feather of Smoke

COOPER AND HIS crew had put up the sail again and were moving well. They were heading for the coast as quickly as possible—whenever it was safe to sail. It was crucial to their survival.

Back in England, Doug Critchley's parents and sister were mourning his loss; Mary Cornish's sister, Eileen, was devastated, as were all the boys' parents. Everyone on the lifeboat had people back home who were mourning—or in the case of the lascars, would be, when news of the disaster reached them.

But now, around four o'clock, they spotted something that, from far away, looked like a ship. Could it be? It was hard to tell. But whatever it was seemed to be sailing in their direction.

As the dot grew larger, Mary could see the outline of a ship, and a fine feather of smoke.

Bohdan Nagorski had crawled under the awning earlier to get some rest. All of a sudden he heard commotion and shouts. Then someone poked his head under the tarp and told him: a ship is sailing in the direction of the boat. And by the angle of its course, it was bound to meet them. Nagorski overcame his fatigue and crawled out to see.

So did the boys. They all jumped up and waved and shouted, even though the ship was too far away to hear them or see them, even through binoculars or a telescope.

Mary Cornish's petticoat, which she had sacrificed on the first day for just this purpose, was run up the mast. It was a flag, an alarm, a signal of distress: Help us!

Father Rory and the children bowed and prayed, saying the Our Father together. Ken picked up his head and made a lot of noise, despite his lack of energy—they all did. They yelled and waved, desperately trying to get the attention of the crew on the ship.

And at this moment Mary Cornish was astonished to remember a recurring dream she had had as a child:

She had been shipwrecked and was adrift in a crowded boat, weak from exhaustion, when a steamer was sighted. The vessel came closer, intent on rescue, and the lifeboat was made fast to its side. Mary had to leap across a gap up to safety, but in her weakness she could not span the distance; she dropped down between steamer and lifeboat into the sea, and lay on the bed of the ocean. She was quite comfortable there, surprised to find that drowning was not more unpleasant.

If only the first part would happen! To be rescued would be a dream—the good part—come true.

Father Rory could see the masts and funnel of a ship on the horizon, and as it came closer, it looked to him to be a merchant ship.

Nagorski judged the ship to be no more than six or seven hundred yards away, a large freighter. They were sailing right toward it.

Cooper and his crew got the lifeboat ready. One of the sailors took down the awning that had sheltered the boys. Worried that the standing poles might get in the way as the boys got onto the ship, the crew pulled those out, too. There was no place to stow them, so they tossed two out of the three into the water. Everyone put on a life preserver.

Cooper explained how the rescue would take place. The ship would be much taller than the lifeboat, so they would be lifted off one by one. Those who were strong enough would climb up rope ladders. But that was unlikely for most of the people on lifeboat 12, five days at sea. The order of rescue would be the children first, then Mary, then Father Rory and Nagorski, and finally all the crew and sailors.

As the ship neared, everyone watched closely. Very soon they would be safe, their ordeal over. Mary exulted. They would be able to stretch their legs! They would be able to have as much water as they wanted!

It was none too soon; many of them were doing poorly. And another storm was brewing, they could all tell. The waves were getting higher, and on the horizon, behind the ship, the clouds were growing darker.

"Hope," wrote poet Emily Dickinson, is the thing with feathers –

> That perches in the soul –
> And sings the tune without the words –
> And never stops – at all –
>
> And sweetest – in the Gale – is heard –
> And sore must be the storm –
> That could abash the little Bird
> That kept so many warm –
>
> I've heard it in the chillest land –
> And on the strangest Sea –

Yet, never, in Extremity,
It asked a crumb – of Me.

....

THE PASSENGERS OF lifeboat 12 had hope on that strange sea. Hope had kept them going these past five days. And now here was a ship, coming toward them. There was nothing to do but wait, their eyes on the fine feather of smoke, hope perched in their souls . . .

And then the unthinkable happened.

The ship turned away.

CHAPTER 26

Darkest Hours

THE PASSENGERS ON lifeboat 12 watched the feather of smoke, of hope, disappear. The ship got smaller and smaller, becoming a smudge, and then a dot, then a pinprick, and then nothing at all, disappearing into the distance, a sad wisp of dream, a phantom rescue ship. Gone.

To this day, no one knows the name of the ship or why it turned away.

Would Mary's childhood nightmare of going to sleep on the ocean floor come true? Disbelief and despair filled her, filled everyone on the boat.

For the first time since the *City of Benares* had been torpedoed, the boys cried.

And then a storm started in earnest.

Disbelief and grief—and a gale's forces. Another windy, wet, freezing-cold night to get through.

This was their darkest hour, their darkest night. The boys were inconsolable. Father Rory summoned his strength and his faith, and he tried something new. Instead of Mary's Bulldog Drummond that night, he told them about a shrine in France, Our Lady of Rocamadour. A hermit is said to be buried there—someone who knew Jesus personally. People make pilgrimages to this shrine, Father Rory told the boys. At the shrine is a bell that sometimes rings by itself. When that happens, it means that somewhere out at sea a person who was saved from drowning has made a vow to visit the shrine.

We will visit the shrine, too, the boys vowed. When we get back to land, we will go to Our Lady of Rocamadour, Father Rory! And with this vow, so the story said, the bell will ring. They will be saved! They will not drown!

Father O'Sullivan was glad the story gave them hope. But, he had to explain, the shrine was far away, in France, and it now was under control of the Nazis.

The boys were not deterred. Tears turned to determination, and with hope in their hearts once again, they made it through that dark and stormy night.

....

MONDAY, THE SIXTH day: though the gale lessened, it continued to rain. It was almost a week since the torpedo hit. A week that they had been at sea in this little boat. With Auntie Mary. Sometimes Father Rory, too, when he was well, or Peard, who swam. And the crew. But mostly Auntie Mary. She was the one.

Back in England, Mary's friends wrote letters to her sister, Eileen. Letters of shock, sympathy, and grief. They wrote about Mary's kindness, how she was someone who took care of others, always. They told how beloved Mary was as a teacher and a friend. How they loved to hear her beautiful piano playing and her charming conversation.

How *of course* she would have given her life in the effort to save others.

"Mary was loved by all who knew her," wrote one friend.

"Mary had friends everywhere and she gave her kindness and her friendship so lavishly," wrote another.

The letters poured in.

"You do not know me but your sister taught me music for seven years and I wanted to let you know how grieved I am for you and how much I shall miss her. Although I was only her pupil she was one of my most valued friends."

"She was . . . large-hearted, stalwart, and I loved her beautiful face and good laughter."

In newspapers, lists of names were printed. The children and the escorts, including Mary Cornish, with her age incorrectly stated as twenty-one. That error gave some of her friends a smidgen of hope: perhaps this was a case of mistaken identity.

And at least one friend wrote in anger: "I can't think what possessed dear Mary to throw her life away like this. I fear my patriotism is very weak. I suppose it was just her amazing generosity. I have never met anyone of such generous sympathy . . . I do hope she died quickly but I suppose we'll never know."

Another friend wrote, "I wish I could say something to comfort you but it is hard to do so, except I think that, in some rather groping way, one does always feel that someone who put as much into life got so much from it as Mary did, does somehow come out victorious."

And, "The only consolation you can have is that she died as she would wish, doing something to help others, but it is so hard for those left."

. . . .

THE BOYS BEGGED Mary for more stories, more Bulldog Drummond. She could barely talk. Her lips were crusted, her mouth dry, her tongue swollen, too.

Not only was her mouth not working very well—neither was her brain. Thoughts were not forming logically.

And yet she talked. She told them stories of Bulldog and Nazis and secret missions and victories. Even she couldn't understand what she was saying. But she kept going. Twice a day.

Earlier, a few days ago, a lifetime ago, she had gotten tired of Bulldog and the Nazis, and she described an English garden, but that didn't go over too well with the boys.

Back to her version of Bulldog Drummond, with a little Richard Hannay mixed in.

Forever.

Sometimes Father Rory led them all in a prayer, though. That was good.

Prayer was needed.

The boys' small bodies were getting smaller.

Ken, Paul, Derek, Howard, Bill, and Fred were in and out of sleep and wakefulness, in and out of thoughts, dreams; they were sad, possibly dying.

They were all so thirsty.

They still sucked their pajama buttons to get their saliva going, and Ken his little lamb, but it didn't really help much. It gave them something to do. But the saliva they made was puny.

And in the water jug, there was not enough water to last much longer.

George Purvis knew the boys needed more water if they were to survive. But he could not give anyone more water than was allotted. A mutiny could erupt.

So the hours went by, or were they minutes?

The sense of time was more blurred than ever on lifeboat 12. The only markers they had were the sun rising and setting, their drops of water in the metal cylinder, and their meals, such as they were. Bulldog.

At least one shipwrecked sailor has reported that you can mark the time out at sea by birds coming or sharks appearing every night at five o'clock.

But the boys on lifeboat 12 saw no sharks. Probably that was a good thing.

No more whales, either. Or if someone saw a whale, it wasn't mentioned. That had been nice, though, for a while, those whales. When was that, two days ago, that they saw the whales? Beautiful sight, but they had to steer away from them because a whale is so big it could topple the boat.

The boys were in and out of sleep, as if sick with a fever, when you don't know what is real and what isn't. And if you're awake or asleep, then you wake up and you know you are awake, how much time has passed? An hour? Two? Or five minutes?

Sonia Bech, on her raft, for only that one long night, said later that she had kept a very good sense of time because she had to work to hold on. She had to pay attention, and that saved her life. It was a long time to cling to a raft. It had been a long time for Beth Cummings and Bess Walder to cling to the overturned lifeboat, for Colin Ryder Richardson to sit in the lifeboat surrounded by dead bodies, for Jack Keeley to hold on to his raft, a long time for all those who survived the night of the torpedo.

Now those survivors were safe and warm. But every day these boys were in more and more danger of dying.

Soon everything would slow down and stop. On the night of the torpedo, children had died not only from drowning but also just from being horribly cold, their organs shutting down one by one. In one night. In hours.

But Ken and Howard and Paul and Fred and Derek and Bill were all still alive. Mary was determined . . .

Howard didn't talk much. He was from Middlesex, outside of London. He was an only child, his parents and grandparents back home grieving for him.

Paul's feet were sore. Trench foot? Frostbite? Both? Paul needed Mary badly; Mary was there.

Time passed.

Or did it?

Drifting in and out of consciousness as they were, the boys had difficulty telling what was real, what were dreams. And time had no real meaning to them. But it did to their bodies. The more hours that passed, the less chance they had to survive.

How do you stop this if you want to get off? Jack had asked, after only one harrowing night at sea.

These boys' bodies were suffering day after day, night after night.

The only way to measure time was by the meals, such as they were. The ship's biscuit came around again. Each boy gave his to Auntie Mary to hold. A sweet slice of peach slipped down their throats. The water, mere drops, not enough. Not nearly enough.

Back into the sleepy states the boys went, nothing to do, nothing to see . . .

And then someone saw land on the horizon. LAND!

LAND!

They all stared—could it be? It sure looked like land.

New hope! LAND, far away, but there, on the horizon!

Robinson Crusoe had found an island. He survived. If they found an island, it wouldn't be home, but they would be off this boat.

There might be food, water.

The passengers of lifeboat 12 went to sleep dreaming of land, of what would happen with the next sunrise.

But not everyone dreamed happily. In the dark of the night, Ken Sparks started screaming. He was delirious, hallucinating, terrified, screaming, screaming, screaming.

Mary and Father Rory held him tight, rocked him.

Eventually he quieted. Mary watched over him. She would not sleep.

Ken would not die on her watch.

CHAPTER 27

Illusions, Delusions, More Nightmares

WHEN DAWN BROKE, there was no land in sight, not even a sliver. The land had been an illusion, one they had all shared. Now all they saw was the open ocean. It was a huge disappointment—not as great as the ship sailing away, but it was a blow.

They were all alone on the vast sea. A speck, a dot that no one could see. But the speck was a boat, and on that boat were forty-six people. Each person had a life, a story, a life worth living and a story worth telling. Would they get to tell it? Would they get to live out their lives? War was raging in other places, on land, on sea. By the time the Second World War was over, more than sixty million people would die. Would these six boys and the others be among them? Sixty million, a number as incomprehensible as the expanse of the ocean.

After the last two days, life seemed but a dream.

There was some good news: the weather was decent again, and Ken was a bit better. But he wasn't good. None of the boys were.

Mary Cornish and Father Rory O'Sullivan, all the adults, were seriously worried about the boys. Bill and Howard, Derek and Ken, Fred and Paul were horribly thirsty. Their limbs and muscles hurt. Their feet were sore. Doug Critchley showed the others how to chafe the boys' feet, and he wrapped one of the boys in his arms, tucking the sore feet under his own shirt.

The boys were getting weaker by the minute. They would drift into the other world, slowly but inevitably, if rescue did not come.

Many of the lascars were in the same state; several of them were lying on the bottom of the boat, barely conscious.

Father Rory suggested to Bohdan Nagorski that the lascars might feel better if they were touched, too. Those who didn't have shoes on were in pain—their feet were red and swollen and covered with sores. Why not paint their feet with iodine? Iodine is used to prevent infection in sores. Nagorski agreed it was a good idea. He found iodine in the boat's first-aid kit and spent almost two hours painting feet and massaging legs. How much it would help, Nagorski didn't know. But it raised the men's spirits and his, too. It made him feel good to be of use.

It was the seventh day.

There was nothing to do but rest. In all of creation, they could see only each other and the vast ocean.

When George Purvis sent the noontime water around, he knew it was the last time they would have water at midday.

He didn't tell anyone, but the water was almost gone.

There would be time for that kind of bad news.

Purvis and Ronnie Cooper were well aware that if they were not rescued in a day or two, people would start to die, the children first.

Nagorski had told the boys he would give them their pocket money when they were rescued. Now Father Rory heard him say he'd double it. Nagorski now was known as the millionaire or even the billionaire.

Thinking about what they would buy once they were rescued—this picked up the boys for a while. Father Rory heard them talking about what they'd drink when they got home, and he became even more thirsty, though he hadn't thought that was possible.

Mary managed to tell some more Bulldog Drummond episodes, though whether they could understand her, she didn't know. She couldn't understand herself.

And then it was night again.

They had made it through another day.

But there was no relief from pain and fear and agony that night.

Paul Shearing became delirious. Mary wanted to rub his feet, but they were so sore that he couldn't stand to have her touch them.

She stayed close and watched helplessly as he became more and more terrified. It was a clear night, and the moonlight was playing a trick on him, shining through the rigging and creating bars. Paul thought he was behind bars, in prison. He rolled from side to side, trying to get out of prison.

But he knew he wasn't actually in prison, and that terrified him even more because he was certain he was going crazy.

He screamed and cried and shouted, his words piercing the silent night: I'm mad, I'm mad, I *know* I'm going mad.

Mary and Rory tried to calm him down. They were terrified themselves. What was happening to this poor boy?

Then word was whispered to them: the others in the boat were getting upset by Paul's screams. Ronnie Cooper warned them to keep Paul quiet.

Cooper knew everyone had to stay calm, to keep control. Their boat had become a community, but at this point everyone was fragile, and the bonds might be, too.

Mary tried to hold Paul close, but when she touched him, he screamed even more. Father Rory sent word to Cooper and Purvis that Paul needed water. Knowing everyone on the boat wanted—and needed—water, Cooper was reluctant. What if this one act of kindness caused a revolt?

But how could they not help the boy? They managed to secretly give Paul a few drops.

Father Rory gave Paul the last rites in case he should die. He spoke in Latin: "Per istam sanctam Unctionem, et suam piissimam misericordiam, indulgeat tibi Dominus quidquid per visum deliquisti. Amen. Per istam sanctam Unctionem, et suam piissimam misericordiam . . ."

To some on the boat, even though they didn't know the words, Father Rory's voice was soothing, peaceful. A certain calm descended.

But Paul was still upset. Harry Peard came to take a look at what was going on. Paul was begging for more water.

Using the toughness he was famous for, Peard told Paul that he would get more water in the morning.

Paul said he wanted it now.

Peard told him: You will get plenty of water when we are rescued. What else is wrong? he demanded.

My feet are cold, Paul answered in a small voice.

Peard yelled at Mary to rearrange the jacket—her own jacket— that was around the boy's feet. She did. Warm now? he said to Paul.

Paul said his feet were still cold. Doug Critchley offered his jacket. Peard took it and covered Paul's feet with that, too.

Paul was still cold.

No, said Peard. You are warm enough. No more. No more yelling. Do you hear? And are your feet warm enough?

Yes, said Paul.

Peard went back to his part of the boat, mumbling about how badly Mary and Father Rory were taking care of the boys.

Miraculously, his tough love worked. Paul calmed down. Ken offered to lie beside him. With his friend next to him, Paul went to sleep, and all was quiet until the morning.

Another disaster averted. There was no mutiny. When the sun rose, everyone, including Paul, was alive.

But they couldn't last much longer. The water jug was almost empty.

CHAPTER 28

And on the Eighth Day. . .

WEDNESDAY, SEPTEMBER 25, dawned bright and clear. The sea was serene, calmer than it had been since the torpedo hit the *Benares* eight days earlier. There was a wind, so Cooper set sail again. The lifeboat was nice and steady, moving well. Mary was relieved: with the boat steadier, the boys would be able to move around a little bit, finally. They could stretch their aching legs; they could breathe some fresh sea air.

Mary had the crew take down the awning so that the boys could sit in the sun. Then she helped them sit with their feet over the side of the lifeboat. Paul was still miserably sick, so Mary kept him lying down. But Ken, Howard, Derek, Bill, and Fred sat with their legs dangling. They would have liked to dive into the water, to refresh themselves, but they weren't strong enough. Instead they watched as Harry Peard stripped down and dove in for his swim. Peard swam alongside the boat for a good long time and came back on board look-ing refreshed and healthy. Much of that was for show. He wanted to keep the boys' spirits up, so he didn't let on that he was in serious pain from badly damaged feet and an injured back.

When it was time for the midday water, Purvis didn't pass around the beaker. All he said was that there wouldn't be water until later.

All the passengers on lifeboat 12 suffered with parched throats, dry and cracked lips, mouths with no saliva. But the meal came: a piece of canned salmon on a ship's biscuit. How could they get down any food? It was nearly impossible. As usual, the boys handed the biscuits to Auntie Mary. But they all managed to choke down the salmon.

There was nothing on board that could satisfy their thirst.

The boys were slipping in and out of wakefulness. Would they just go to sleep and . . . ?

Rescue seemed impossible.

. . . .

AT ONE IN the afternoon Ken Sparks yelled.

He had seen something in the sky.

"Sunderland!" he shouted, pointing to the west. Later Ken wouldn't even remember it was he who spotted the plane. Or that he stood up and started signaling it.

It was hard for anyone on the boat to believe at first that it really was a plane. They'd seen what they thought were planes before, only to watch them turn into gulls. And what if the plane didn't notice them—or passed them by?

The steamer had turned away. Would the plane?

But no.

It *was* a plane. A Sunderland seaplane.

And the pilot had seen the lifeboat.

Almost everyone on the boat—everyone who was well

enough—was sitting straight, looking up. Signaling, waving. Smiling.

The plane circled around them two or three times. The crew hoisted Mary's petticoat up the mast again. Ken waved his shirt. The seaplane signaled a Morse code message with an Aldis lamp. We are from the Royal Australian Air Force, they signaled, a member of the Sunderland Division 10 Squadron.

Navy signalman Johnny Mayhew answered with semaphore signs, using some of the Indians' turbans as flags: We are from the *City of Benares*.

Lifeboat 12 was a mere speck on the great Atlantic Ocean.

But it was a speck that had been spotted.

....

"THE PLANE DROPPED a smoke flare with instructions to set it off when the rescue ship was in sight. He then made off," Ronnie Cooper would later report. Low on fuel, the Royal Australian Air Force plane sped off to alert its relief plane of the lifeboat's location.

Cooper lowered the sail so they wouldn't move. He wanted to maintain their position so the rescuers could easily find them. They would just sit and wait for help.

About an hour later, they saw a plane again. A Sunderland. It looked to Cooper like the same one, although it was the relief plane, from the British Royal Air Force. Out of the plane dropped a parcel. They retrieved it and read the note attached: a rescue ship was coming. It was forty miles away.

In the parcel was food. Beans in tomato sauce, more canned salmon and peaches. There was no water. They desperately needed water.

But the food would do for now, and they feasted on it, "draining every drop of peach juice and tomato sauce out of the tins," Mary said later.

The passengers begged Purvis for water. Couldn't they have some water now that rescue was on the way? There was some left on the boat. They were so thirsty. But Purvis had to refuse. They weren't rescued yet. He needed to hold on to the last of the water—just in case the rescue ship did not come.

A fight could have broken out. But during these eight days at sea the people on lifeboat 12 *had* built a strongly knit community based on goodwill and shared experience. And success. Purvis had kept them alive this far . . .

And a ship was coming.

One of the sailors pulled out a harmonica, and those who could, sang.

Meanwhile, the pilot had flown back to the warship and saw it was on the wrong course.

Finally, at 4:30 p.m., the passengers on lifeboat 12 saw the destroyer coming. There was a plane flying above it, guiding the rescuers to the little craft. "I flew across the ship indicating the direction it should take," the RAF pilot reported. "The warship altered course and followed."

Royal Navy destroyer HMS Anthony *arrives to rescue the passengers of lifeboat 12.* [Wikimedia Commons/Imperial War Museum]

Within half an hour, HMS *Anthony* was alongside the lifeboat, and the rescue began. Each boy was lifted onto the destroyer, clutching a tin of sweetened condensed milk. The last few days they hadn't been able to swallow the milk—it was too thick to get down their parched throats. But the boys wanted to bring home a souvenir for their mothers. Mothers who thought they were dead.

And so they would.

Mary Cornish needed help up the rope ladder, and once aboard, she had to be carried belowdecks. After eight days of very little sleep, of so much sacrifice, she was a wreck. She had given everything she had to the boys. She had saved them with stories. Now her mind wasn't working. She couldn't even figure out how to get undressed or dressed. She could barely move. But she was alive.

Some of the lascars were extremely weak, too. They also had to be lifted aboard. One of the men was seriously ill and died shortly after being rescued.

Everyone else on the lifeboat survived. The boys would all need time to get better. Some of them would take longer than others. Paul's feet were the worst, and he would write to Mary two years later that he had to go back to the hospital because his toes hurt.

But now, on the *Anthony*, the boys were alive and, finally, warm. They had beds to sleep in and food to eat, and water to drink. They were on their way home.

. . . .

Opposite: *Sailors help the lifeboat 12 survivors onto the rescue ship.*
[Shutterstock]

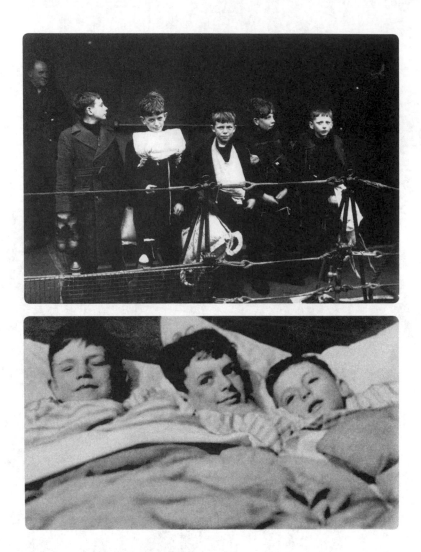

BACK IN ENGLAND, Eileen, Mary's sister, received a telegram: MISS MARY CORNISH, SAFE AND WELL. The *Anthony* crew arranged for Doug Critchley to call Liverpool. Hello, Dad, he said. His father put Doug's sister on the phone to make sure it wasn't a joke.

Top: *Survivors Ken Sparks, Howard Claytor, Fred Steels, Derek Capel, and Bill Short on the HMS* Anthony. *[Shutterstock]* • Above: *Fred, Derek, and Bill, safe, warm, and comfortable in a real bed after so many cold nights on the lifeboat in the open sea.* [Shutterstock]

Father Rory O'Sullivan learned his obituary had been published. He would carry it in his pocket for a very long time. His real obituary would not be written for another sixty-seven years.

Ken's, Fred's, Paul's, and Howard's parents got the great news that they would have their sons back.

Derek's and Bill's parents learned that one of their sons would return. But of course they would never get over the loss of Peter and Alan.

In a few days, when Bill Short saw his mother, his first words to her would be "Mummy, I haven't got Peter for you."

Years later Derek Capel would talk about the loss of his brother, Alan, and confess that he never hugged anyone again, not even his own child.

. . . .

Mary Cornish and Bohdan Nagorski on the HMS Anthony, *with Fred Steels and Derek Capel (in profile).* [Shutterstock]

AS THEY HEADED back to Britain, washed and fed and looked after by the ship's doctor, the passengers of lifeboat 12 found out that they were among the few survivors from the *City of Benares*.

Mary Cornish learned of the terrible fate of Gussie Grimmond and her sisters and brothers and the vast majority of the CORB children. Mary would learn that her friend Sybil had died. Of the 90 CORB children, only 13 survived; 77 had died. Of the 10 escorts, 6 had died. Of the 91 paying passengers, 51 had died; at least 4 of those were children. Of the crew, 91 survived; 124 had died. Overall, of the 406 people aboard the *Benares*, 258 died; 148 survived.

Even as the British press rallied around Mary Cornish as a hero, which she certainly was, and even as she rejoiced that her boys—Ken, Fred, Paul, Howard, Derek, and Bill—would all go home to their parents, she was devastated by the enormity of the loss.

CHAPTER 29

A Watery Grave

IN WARTIME PEOPLE expect deaths, even civilian deaths. But the parents of the children on the *Benares* had sent them on the ship to save their lives.

As the last survivors were reunited with their families, the parents who lost children were just beginning to cope with this unfathomable tragedy. When Hannah and Eddie Grimmond talked to the press about the horrible loss of their five children, Eddie Grimmond said that he wanted to fight for England: "This is not war. It is sheer and cold-blooded murder, and all I ask is for a front-line job."

Hannah agreed. "If Hitler thinks he can beat us this way he made a mistake," she said.

Eddie was denied a fighting job, but he got a position in the photography department of the Royal Air Force.

Even with this tragedy, one more ship with CORB children sailed. The *Nova Scotia* left Liverpool on September 21. The *Benares* had already been sunk, but the news hadn't been released yet.

The *Nova Scotia* set sail before lifeboat 12 was rescued. The convoy it was in was also torpedoed.

Although the *Nova Scotia* itself was not hit, five other ships were sunk. The *Nova Scotia* passengers were ordered to their lifeboat stations, but the ship sailed on and arrived safely in Canada with twenty-nine CORB children and two escorts. No children died. But that was the last ship to carry CORB children away from Britain. Children who were already living abroad stayed, but the children who had yet to be evacuated remained home. Their lives, in most cases, would go on normally, though there would still be many wartime tragedies.

Alan Francis, ten, lived in Wembley, where Ken Sparks and his friend Terence Holmes were from. Alan's father was a policeman from the city of London, and early in the war Mr. Francis had brought home steel helmets for the family to wear. Like other wartime children, Alan carried his gas mask always. He and his family collected Air Raid Precaution cigarette cards. They followed the instructions on the cards, and pasted crisscrosses of "stout" paper on the windows as a precaution against flying glass.

The boys were excited to be on a Royal Navy ship, and the Anthony *sailors were thrilled to have them.* [Shutterstock]

Alan watched airplanes in the sky, as so many of the boys did, and could tell them all apart. He collected shrapnel.

Back when his school passed out the CORB information, he was excited. He wanted his parents to send him and his younger brother, Robin, six. Robin wanted to go, too. It would be an adventure. But after discussing it, their parents decided to keep their sons at home.

During those first weeks of September, bombs fell over their neighborhood. It was a scary time, for sure, but when Alan heard about the ship that got torpedoed, it seemed the right choice that he had stayed home. All the children from his school who were on the *Benares* had died. All six of them. Two were his classmates—Henry Smoolovitch and Bruce Hillyard.

When Alan went to school, he stared at their empty desks. Those boys would never come back. Nor would the others in his school.

Six empty desks.

Soon after Ken Sparks and the other lifeboat 12 boys were rescued, Alan's house was bombed. He and his brother and father survived. But his mother, lying next to his father under the dining room table, was crushed to death.

It could have been Alan. It could have been his father or his brother. It could have been all of them. Or none of them.

Why does death choose some and not others? Why did some people survive the torpedo and the sinking of the *Benares*, and not others?

The parents who sent their children on the trip had had every reason to believe the ship would get to Canada safely. As it turned out, the children who survived the torpedo lived through the war. It is impossible to know if any of those who died on the ship would have been killed in a bombing raid, but in retrospect, it seemed that they might have been safer at home.

People started to write and read reports and talk about what had happened. If only the warships hadn't left. If only Captain Nicoll had prevailed and the *Benares* had sailed on ahead, faster. If only the storm had prevented the U-boat from launching the torpedoes. If only there hadn't been a storm and the lifeboats had launched easily. If only the children hadn't been in their pajamas. If only . . . All these *if only*s did not matter. Not to these parents.

In the month or two after they lost their children, some of the parents wrote to the Ellerman City Line asking for a favor.

"Dear Sirs," wrote Mary and Robert Dixon from Sunderland, "owing to the tragic loss of our only daughter Maureen Dixon in the *City of Benares*, we were wondering if you could supply us with a picture of the above vessel. It would be very comforting if we could see where our little darling spent the last 5 days of her life."

Maureen Dixon had been in Mary Cornish's group. Mary had described her as small and scrappy, with a zest for living. Maureen was ten years old. She had written a card to her parents from the school before they got on the ship, giving her location as "Somewhere in England," obeying the rule not to give away a location lest the enemy found out. "I am very happy," she said. "Don't worry we arrived safely. We are in a lovely hostel . . . We had tea as soon as we got here. Lots of Love xxxxxx Maureen."

George Crawford lost his son, George Jr. He had been a hero that night, losing his life when he'd pulled Louis Walder onto the lifeboat. He was thirteen years old.

"Dear Sirs," Mr. Crawford wrote, "Excuse my taking the liberty of writing you, but I am given to understand that you have a Book giving photos, etc. [of the *City of Benares*]. "You will appreciate no doubt my desire to secure such a book when I inform you that my only son was lost when the above vessel was torpedoed recently."

Mr. Crawford had gotten some postcards, but he wanted "more elaborate information."

Ellerman Lines sent a brochure to George's father—they sent brochures to whoever asked. Mr. Crawford wrote back, thanking them for the favor: "I much appreciate this kindness on your part."

Eleanor Wright had survived the night. She told reporters of George's heroism, and a month later she also wrote to Ellerman Lines: "As you will most probably be aware, I am a survivor from the child evacuee ship S.S. City of Benares. I am writing to ask a favour of you. Could you please supply me with a booklet of the ship, as I wish to show my friends the beautiful ship on which I was being conveyed to Canada." After her initial interviews, Eleanor stopped talking to reporters. And years later, when the other survivors organized reunions, she did not answer or attend. Even for the survivors, the experience was devastating.

Beryl Myatt was one of the seventy-seven CORB children who

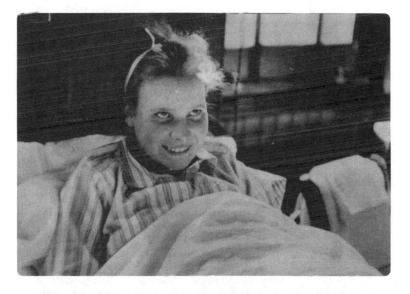

Eleanor Wright, happy to be alive. [Shutterstock]

died. Like so many of the others, we don't know much about her. We don't know about her days on the ship, or how she died. We cannot tell her whole story. But we know she was beloved. She was nine years old, her parents' only child. They had sent her to Canada to live with relatives. They started to miss her as soon as she left, chasing her departure with letters to her. When she died, her parents held a memorial service for her and made donations to a children's fund in her name. But they needed to do more. Her father called the CORB office in London to ask whether a ship could drop a wreath in her memory as near as possible to where the *Benares* went down.

Elspeth Davies, the CORB welfare director, wrote back to Beryl's mother, "I have been making inquiries and am told that in time of war, ships can never tell which course the Navy will require them to follow, and that very rarely do two ships go the same way. So I am afraid it would not be possible to ask any ship to do this for you."

Elspeth Davies worked at CORB throughout the war, since so many children had already been placed in other countries. Much later, long after the war ended, she is reported to have said that sending children away from Great Britain was a mistake.

Beryl Myatt's parents donated some of her things to the Imperial War Museum in London: her tooth-brushing card; her Mickey Mouse Club card; a report she did for school on how a plant grows; the CORB forms they had to fill out; and the packing list for the trip, with check marks next to the items they had packed for their daughter. Also in the file are many notes written to her parents after her death, as well as the letter about the wreath.

Elspeth Davies ended her letter to Beryl's mother with this heart-wrenching piece of advice: "You will have to think of the whole sea as poor little Beryl's grave. She belongs to a very gallant company of people whose grave is the sea."

← Chummy
sends his love.
This is his paw
mark.

73 Penecroft Crescent,
Hillingdon,
Middsex,
England
21st September 1940.

Our Dearest Beryl,

This is our second letter to you
since you set out on your big
adventure Dear, and we suppose you
were very surprised when you arrived
at Auntie Emmies to find a letter and
your Dandy and Sunny Stories waiting
there for you. We will send them each week.

We expect that you enjoyed
your voyage on the boat across
the wide Atlantic Ocean, and
your long journey on the
train to Winnipeg. We don't
suppose you saw any icebergs
during your voyage across, as it
would hardly be quite cold enough
at this time of the year.

Letter to Beryl from her parents. It arrived in Canada; she did not.
[Imperial War Museum, photo by author]

THOSE FROM THE SS *City of Benares* who share a watery grave:

Ala-Ud-Din Abdul
Isamil Adam
Sheikh Adam
Jamal Ahmad
Sheikh Ismail Sheikh Ahmad
Janet Roberts Aitcheson
Ajm-Ud-Din
Karim Ali
Mubarak Ali
Allah
Patricia Allen
Hashim Alli
Khotu Amin
Sheikh Faqir Amin
Sheikh Amjad
Emily Eliza Armes
Jane Prue Armes
Hugh H. Asher
Madaz Azad
Aziz
Aziz-Ur-Rahman
Usman Baba
Sulaiman Badr-Ud-Din
Babu
Annie Bailey
Robert Baker
Rahim Bakhsh
Bakr-Ud-Din
James Baldwin-Webb
Daud Balla
Ibrahim Balla
Sheikh Nur-Ud-Din Bapu
Kathleen Beatrice Barrett
Florence Barton

Edna Doreen Beesley
Phyllis Eileen Beesley
Vera Ellen D. Beesley
Bhakua
Abbas Bhickoo
George W. H. Blake
Michael John Brooker
Gertrude Helen Brown
Marion Dick Buchanan
Alice Mary Bulmer
Enid Evelyn Butlin
James Reginald Came
Lewis Victor Came
Helen Robertson Miller
    Campbell
Alan John Capel
Beryl Irene Carr
Cecil Frances Muriel Carr
Derek Stanley Carr
Ernest Charnock
Michael John Chase
Sheila Astrid Chase
Ramaswami Chikappa
Frank Clifford Choat
Gretchen Coleman
Christina Sharp Cook
George Geoffrey Crawford
Pauline Mary Crawley
Sheila Anne Crawley
Florence Alexandra
    Croasdaile
John Lawrence Croasdaile
Patricia Joan Croasdaile
James Cuthbertson

Silvester D'Costa
Vivian Cynthia Dadds
Muhammad Sheikh Daud
Dorothy Wyatt Deane
Maud Goringe Deane
Sheikh Hasan Dharmu
Usman Dhondu
Dr. Nadirshah Jamshedji
    Dhondy
Maureen Margaret Dixon
Phyllis Elizabeth
Barbara Ruth Fairhead
Alister Fairweather
Razaq Faqir
Manuel Fernandes
Roque S. Fernandes
Anne Dorothea Fleetwood-
    Hesketh
Duncan Fletcher
Jean Forster
Dorothy Galliard
James Gemmell
Abdul Ghani
Aman Abdul Ghani
John C. Gibbeson
Sybil Gilliat-Smith
William Golightly
Christopher Robin Goodfellow
Derek Charles Goodfellow
Zygmunt Gralinski
Ruby Isobel Grierson
Augusta E. Grimmond
Constance J. Grimmond
Edward Grimmond Jr.
Leonard A. Grimmond
Violet C. Grimmond
Maurice Groberman

Hirsch Benjamin Heinrich
    Guggenheim
Emily Guggenheim
Muhammad Gulab
Muhammad Gulab
Abdul Haq
James Wilfred Harrington
Patricia Doreen Harrington
Helen Harris
Nellie Hicks
Maud Gladys Hillman
Bruce John Hillyard
Jeffrey Hillyard
Tom Hodgson
Terence Brian Holmes
William Hurwitz
Husain
Muhammad Husain
Sheikh Husain
Edgar Robert Hutchings
Abdullah Ibrahim
Muhammad Ibrahim
Sheikh Muhammad Sheikh
    Ibrahim
Emily Blanca von Ingersleben
Joan Anne Florence Irving
Sharif Sheikh Ismail
Shaukat Ismail
Sheikh Ali Ismail
Muhammad Jafar
Sheikh Muhammad Jan
Jhani
Alfonso Jose
Karl Jungmann
Sheikh Kalu
Sheikh Karim
Joyce Mary Keeley
Hasan Khamis

Jafar Khan Haidar Khan

Muhammad Khan

Faridun Khosrovy

Sheikh Ali Khotu

Rev. William Henry King

Sheikh Labhu

Margaret Ladyman

Lilian Lambert

Jeno Lanyi

Latif

Abdul Latif

John Lazarus

Derek Leigh

Piedade C. Leitao

Freda Leuenberger

Robert W. Livingstone

Margaret Eleanor Lloyd

Nesta Lloyd

Peter John Lloyd

Garath Lunt

William Smith Macfarquhar

Edmond Mackinnon

Donald Macrae

Abdul Majid

Audrey Mansfield

Ismail Mansur

Harry Marriott

Charles Marshall

William McLachlan

Mustand Mian

Robin Miller

John C. Mitchell

Philip Langford Mollard

William Robert "Bobby" Moon

Aileen Sybil Moss

Marion Audrey Moss

Rita Ann Moss

Muhammad

Daud Muhammad

Husain Muhammad

Sheikh Husain Sheikh
    Muhammad

Sher Muhammad

Muhib

Audrey Muncey

Ailsa Burgess Murphy

Francis Money Graham
    Murphy

Beryl Myatt

Nazru Muhammad Nayki

Nazir

Landles Nicoll

Dorothy Sheila Nolan

Patricia Nolan

Sheikh Nur

Rudolph Olden

Ika Olden

Benedic Palma

Panchkori

Panchu

Panna

John Pemberton

Espexian Pereira

Diana Pine

Eileen Emma Maud Pine

Rodger James Poole

Charles Horace Pugh

Donald James Pugh

John Albert Pugh

Ali Sahib Qadir

Ramaswami Ramchandra

Laszlo Raskai

Abdul Razaq

Abdul Razaq

Anita Mary Rees

William Eric Rees

Michael Rennie

John Roberts

Colenso Mackenzie Rodda

Roshan

Layton George Ryman

Sheikh Ahmad Bawa Sahib

Ganpat Sakharam

Muhammad Shafi

Muhammad Shakir

Peter Short

Dorothy Winifred Smith

Edith Smith

Irene Smith

Henry Smoolovitch

Soria

James Thomas Spencer

Joan Margaret Spencer

John Onslow Spencer-Davies

Rosemary Winified Spencer-Davies

Kurt Lowe Stern

Abdul Subhan

Rangaswami Subramani

Sulaiman

Ismail Sultan

James Swales

Frank Symon

Ali Taj-Ud-Din

Anthony Ralph Taylor

June Margaret Taylor

Marion Winifred Thorne

Sheikh Ahmad Kamal Ud-Din

Darasat Ullah

Shafi Ullah

Taimas Ullah Azam Ullah

Betty Unwin

Abdur Rahman Usman

Sheikh Abbas Usman

Sheikh Usman

Agnes Wallace

Gordon Walsh

Ann Jordeson Watson

Thomas William Watson

Ethel Martha Wilde

Peter John Willis

Bertha Sproull Wilson

Dorothy Gertrude Wood

B. Margaret Zeal

Bertha Zoond

AFTER THE VOYAGE

The Lifeboat 12 boys were treated like heroes when they landed in Scotland. They were given kilts and books and keys to the city. They kept in touch with Mary Cornish after they got home. They wrote Auntie Mary letters, sent her holiday cards, wedding and birth announcements. And when she died in 1964, they sent condolence notes to her sister, Eileen. Remarkably, **Derek Capel**, **Bill Short**, **Ken Sparks**, and **Fred Steels** served in the Royal Navy. Even though his feet were severely damaged, **Paul Shearing** went into the army. These five Lifeboat 12 "boys" lived a long time.

Letters from the Lifeboat 12 boys to Mary. [Courtesy of Maggie Paterson, photograph by author]

Mary Cornish was awarded the Medal of the Order of the British Empire. A card sent with cartons of cigarettes to servicemen called *Heroic Deeds of the War* featured Mary's face and the tale of her heroism on the *City of Benares* and lifeboat 12. Mary told a reporter her story for a book entitled *Atlantic Ordeal*. In 1956, Mary Cornish and Father Rory O'Sullivan were reunited with their boys on the Wilfred Pickles television show. Beth Cummings tuned in and afterward wrote to Auntie Mary to say how happy she was to see her again.

Beth Cummings and **Bess Walder** stayed lifelong close friends. More than that—they became family. Beth introduced Bess to her older brother Geoffrey, and Bess married him. Bess became a teacher and often talked about her experiences being torpedoed on the *City of Benares*.

Father Rory O'Sullivan died a month before his ninety-ninth birthday. After the *Benares*, he served as a military chaplain during World War II and was a beloved priest in France for the rest of his life. He wrote a memoir called *Join the Navy? Get Torpedoed First!*

Bohdan Nagorski moved to the United States and continued to work in the shipping business. He wrote a chapter in a book about his experiences in lifeboat 12, and his nephew Tom wrote a book for adults about the *City of Benares*. Bohdan lived to be ninety-six years old.

Colin Ryder-Richardson was given a King's Commendation for brave conduct in the Merchant Navy. Colin fought—and won—a battle with cancer, living to age eighty-three. His red life jacket is on display at the Egham Museum, near his hometown in Surrey, England.

Members of the crew were given commendations and medals, including **Ramjam Buxoo**, **Ronnie Cooper**, **George Purvis**, and **Abdul Subhan**.

The Bech family went back to their seaside house and lived out the war there. They all settled nearby with their families. Sonia became a schoolteacher; she still goes to the village school to tell about her experience on the *City of Benares* and the life raft. As of this writing, she is ninety years old and lives with her cat, Victor Sylvester. Her husband, brother, and sister all died in 2016.

Jack Keeley and **John McGlashan** met fifty years after the torpedo. It was the first time they actually talked, since McGlashan wasn't able to speak on the raft.

At age seven, **John Baker** was the youngest survivor. When he got back to Southall, his parents sent him away again, this time to a small village, so he could be away from the bombing. But John refused to stay there, and his parents brought him home. John married and became an engineer, designing Rolls-Royce airplane engines.

Heinrich "Ajax" Bleichrodt served as the commander of two other U-boats and was awarded the Knight's Cross with Oak Leaves. He was held for war crimes after the war ended, but there was not enough evidence to go to trial. According to Rolf Hilse, Ajax suffered a mental collapse when he heard there were one hundred children on board the *Benares*.

Rolf Hilse was taken prisoner of war in England. He married an English woman and lived in England for the rest of his life.

Commander Hugh Crofton Simms died in 1942 when German planes bombed the ship he was commanding. His son, Blake, was only a few years old. When he grew up, Blake helped to organize reunions of the survivors of the *City of Benares*.

Because of the terrible loss of lives in the *City of Benares* disaster, the Royal Navy made a lifesaving change. Starting a few weeks later, all convoys had a designated rescue ship. If a vessel was torpedoed or damaged, the rescue ship would stay to save as many people as possible. What a difference that would have made on the night of September 17.

The *City of Benares* lies at the bottom of the ocean. A British company attempting to retrieve gold and diamonds from World War II ships has promised to leave the ship untouched, as it is a grave.

For more, please visit *DeborahHeiligman.com*.

The author with Sonia Bech Williams in the church where Sonia was married. [Jonathan Weiner]

THANK YOU

Many people helped me with this book—in ways I have never experienced before. Not only colleagues, friends, and family but also friends of friends and complete strangers (some of whom became friends). In email and in person, people went out of their way to help, responding quickly and diving deep into their files, their minds, their hearts. This story seems to bring out the best in people, which is a beautiful thing.

My thanks go first and foremost to my editor Laura Godwin, who showed me a fuzzy photograph on her phone of Colin's custom-made life jacket. Thank you, Laura, for starting me on this journey and for staying right by my side as I rode the stormy waves up and down. You captained this ship with brilliance, kindness, and humor. And not a few dog photos. Julia Sooy was right there, too, always, not only as an editor but also as a friend. She threw me a life belt whenever I needed it (often), gave me help above and beyond the call of duty, and also supplied delicious vegetarian recipes.

Thanks to everyone at Macmillan for helping me create this book and for getting it to readers. Thank you to what-would-we-do-without-her managing editor Jennifer Healey, who kept us all in line and on time (more or less) and gave me the best copyeditor and fact-checker in the universe, Sherri Schmidt. Once again, Jen and Sherri, I owe you big. Thanks to Janet Renard for excellent proofreading, and to Tom Nau for your production prowess. Thank you to Patrick Collins, art director, and to Raphael Geroni for the design of the book. Lawrence Lee created the illustrations.

Jean Feiwel, Jonathan Yaged, Allison Verost, Jennifer Edwards, and Angus Killick run the Macmillan Children's Book enterprise, and they do it with verve and smarts. I am so grateful to be in your hands for my author journey.

Macmillan School and Library team—thank you for your support, always. Lucy Del Priore, Katie Halata, Kristen Luby, and Melissa Croce, I'm so glad you're here again with your oars in the water.

And to marketing and publicity, how can you be so much fun and so good at your jobs? Thanks to Kathryn Little and Johanna Kirby and to my cabinmates, Teresa Ferraiolo, Brittany Pearlman, and Molly Brouillette. I will be sending desserts. Lots of desserts.

Thank you to the sales team, headed by Mark Von Bargen, Jess Brigman, Rebecca Schmidt, Sofrina Hinton, and Taylor Armstrong. And to Kristin Dulaney, Catherine Kramer, and Jordan Winch for getting my books to more readers. And to Mariel Dawson and Gaby Salpeter for getting the word out far and wide.

A huge thank-you to my agent, Susan Ginsburg, who reads my drafts, weathers my storms, feeds me warm eggplant, gives me travel advice, makes me laugh, and most of all *gets* me. I am one lucky author. Thank you also to Stacy Testa and Catherine Bradshaw and to everyone at Writers House. And to Dobbie Combs for my website and more.

Working on the book, I relied as much as I could on interviews with survivors and relatives of survivors. I was lucky to do a few of them myself, but most were conducted years ago by Lyn Smith for the Imperial War Museum. I am so grateful to her for asking the questions I would have asked, and to the Imperial War Museum for making the interviews available to me and to the public. They are treasures. Lyn, thank you, too, for your books and for answering my questions in email.

Jennifer Robertson, Assistant Curator of Maritime History, National Museums Liverpool, Merseyside Maritime Museum, has been a godsend for this book, answering questions first in emails, then in person, and again in emails. Thank you, Jen, for showing me around the museum and the dock, and for sharing your files with me, and for your expertise and the many, many questions you answered. Thank you, too, to Ian Murphy, Deputy Director Merseyside Maritime Museum, for his help with this book.

Reverend Alan Walker of St. Jude's on the Hill responded immediately to an email with much information about Michael Rennie, and then welcomed my husband and me to his church in North London. And he helped me unlock the key so I could hear the IWM interview with Rolf Hilse.

Thank you to so many people at the Imperial War Museum, especially: Jenny Waldman, Richard Hughes, John Delaney, Gemma Brown, Megan Denz, and Maria Rollo.

Librarians and archivists are heroes. Thank you to the librarians at the British Library, the New York Public Library, Columbia University library, and to the archivists at the University of Glasgow, the National Archives, and at Keble College.

Thanks to Martha Pichey, Lucinda Montefiore, and James Stephenson for connecting me with material I would not have seen otherwise.

For help with understanding what happened to the children who died from exposure, I am indebted to Dr. Will Standiford.

In my quest to find first-person accounts of lascars, many people tried to help. Even though we didn't turn up anything (yet), I am grateful for the advice, consultations, legwork, and research. First, to Ankur Paliwal, for spending many hours researching in archives and talking to people in India. Thank you for trying so hard, and for reading the parts of the book about the lascars. I hope one day we will be able to revise this book to include an unearthed story. Thank you to Esha Day, Malavika Vyawahare, and Ruhi Kandhari for your research and help in India and here. The following people pointed me in various directions and gave me leads: Nikhil Bhojwani, Professor Gayatri Chakravorty Spivak, Amitav Gosh, Barbara Grant, Sameera Kahn, Anthony Lane, Shahida Rahman, Sree Sreenivasan, Ansar Ahmed Ullah of the Swadhinata Trust, Professor Fleur D'Souza, Commodore B K Mohanti of the Lascar War Memorial, Commodore Mohan Narayan, and Rozina Visram. I've probably missed a few; forgive me.

Thank you to Steve and Gail Rubin, Professor Jeff Bolster, and Chris Kerr for answering my questions about ships and sailing. Thank you to Ruta Sepetys, Eddie Bridges, and Carol Bommarito for answering my questions, and to Professor Volker Berghahn, Professor Paul Kennedy,

Professor Pablo Piccato, and Professor Adam Tooze for your help answering my questions about history and World War II. Thanks to librarian Allie Bruce for letting me pepper her Bank Street students with questions.

Thank you to Kathleen Gill of the Sunderland Volunteer Life Brigade for putting me in touch with Bill Short, with whom I spoke just before he died. And to the Egham Museum, which holds Colin's life jacket.

Thank you to Judy Grimmond Rogers for answering what questions she could about the Grimmond family; to Bill Richards, Chairman of the Christ's Hospital Heritage Committee, for helping me with research about Michael Rennie; to Adelaide Morris for introducing me to *Drift* and talking about perils both at sea and at the writing desk. And to Michael Stern, David Fleischer, and Sandy Tipping, who consulted about the all-clear signal.

Thank you to Sarah Ryder Richardson for sharing her wonderful memories of her father, Colin, and for taking photographs of the life jacket. And thank you to Julian Ryder Richardson for his memories and for answering my many questions, and to Jill Ryder Richardson, Colin's first wife, for sharing what she knew about his experience.

Thanks to Maggie Paterson, Mary Cornish's niece-in-law, for her memories, for letting me see Mary's piano and hold her baton, and especially for letting me look through Eileen Cornish Paterson's suitcase full of letters, telegrams, cards, and memorabilia. They are priceless and added to the book in so many ways.

Thank you to Stephanie Hernandez, a stranger on the train to Liverpool, for lending me a charger for my laptop when I asked where I could buy one.

My trip to England to see the suitcase and visit Sonia Bech Williams and John Baker was the highlight of writing this book. Special thanks to Beverly Gee, who made so much of it possible with her brains and her generosity, and to Nathaniel and Francis Gee for their warmth and hospitality.

Thanks to these wonderful people who are not only great friends and family but who also read drafts of the book: Barbara Kerley, Nancy

Sandberg, Karan Singh, Benjamin Weiner, Jonathan Weiner, and Aaron Zinger.

Thanks also to the friends and family without whom I would let go of the keel: Laurie Halse Anderson, Judy Blundell, Marfé Ferguson Delano, Lucy Frank, Daphne Benedis-Grab, Marthe Jocelyn, Eva Kosta, Susan Kuklin, Ann Martin, Lock McKelvy, Xotchil Medina, Elizabeth Partridge, Margo Rabb, Natalie Standiford, Rebecca Stead, Katie Walsh, Eric Weiner, Ken Wright, and Sarah Zinger.

Last and most: thank you to Sonia Bech Williams and John Baker for talking to me, for welcoming me into your hearts, homes, and lives.

John Baker does not like to talk about the event and his tragedy, and yet he graciously agreed to talk with me, and has continued to do so. Thank you, John, for your courage, for opening up to me as much as you could, for hosting us in Derby, and for continuing conversations about the *City of Benares* and life. I look forward to many more FaceTime chats.

Sonia Bech Williams welcomed me and my husband into her home for five days. She told me many stories and let me look through her scrapbook, hold her jewelry box. Together we went to her childhood home. (And thank you to John and Jeanne Andrews, who let us barge in on them and walk through the house!)

Those five days with the eighty-nine-year-old Sonia changed our lives. When we asked her how she kept so cheerful, even in the face of illness and loss, she said, "I was torpedoed, I am resilient." We are, all of us, torpedoed in some way, and Jonathan and I have embraced Sonia not only as a dear friend but also as a role model. Thank you, Sonia, for your heart, your hospitality, your time, and your vitality.

None of what I do would be possible without the love and support of my husband, Jonathan Weiner. I am so grateful to be on this voyage with him.

SELECT BIBLIOGRAPHY

BOOKS

(Those with an asterisk are suitable for younger readers.)

*Adams, Simon. *Winston Churchill*. London: Franklin Watts, 2003.

Atkinson, Kate. *A God in Ruins*. New York: Little Brown, 2015.

*——. *Life After Life*. New York: Little, Brown, 2013.

Barker, Ralph. *Children of the Benares: A War Crime and Its Victims*. London: Methuen, 1987.

Bergvall, Caroline. *Drift*. Callicoon, NY: Nightboat Books, 2014.

Birkwood, Ilene. *The Second Torpedo*. Self-published, 2012.

Bradley, Kimberly Brubaker. *The War That Saved My Life*. New York: Penguin, 2015.

*—— —. *The War I Finally Won*. New York: Penguin, 2017

Buchan, John. *The Thirty-Nine Steps*. 1915; reprint, Boston: Houghton Mifflin, 1943.

Clayton, Tim, and Phil Craig. *Finest Hour: The Battle of Britain*. London: Hodder and Stoughton, 1999; New York: Touchstone, 2002.

Cleave, Chris. *Everyone Brave Is Forgiven*. New York: Simon & Schuster, 2016.

Crane, Stephen. "The Open Boat." In *Stephen Crane: Prose and Poetry*, pp. 885–909. New York: Library of America, 1984.

*Defoe, Daniel. *The Life and Adventures of Robinson Crusoe*. London: Penguin, 1965.

Fethney, Michael. *The Absurd and the Brave: CORB—The True Account of the British Government's World War II Evacuation of Children Overseas*. Sussex, UK: Book Guild, 2000.

*Foreman, Michael. *War Boy: A Wartime Childhood*. London: Pavilion, 2006.

García Márquez, Gabriel. *The Story of a Shipwrecked Sailor*. Translated by Randolph Hogan. New York: Knopf, 1986.

Gardiner, Juliet. *Wartime: Britain 1939–1945*. London: Headline Books, 2004.

Harrisson, Tom, and Charles Madge, eds. *War Begins at Home*. London: Chatto & Windus, 1940. Mass Observation Online.

Huxley, Elspeth. *Atlantic Ordeal: The Story of Mary Cornish*. New York: Harper & Brothers, 1942.

Lane, Tony. *The Merchant Seamen's War*. Manchester, UK: Manchester University Press, 1990.

Lord, Walter. *A Night to Remember*. New York: Henry Holt, 2005. Audiobook.

Mann, Jessica. *Out of Harm's Way: The Wartime Evacuation of Children from Britain*. London: Headline, 2005.

*McNeile, Cyril. *Bull-Dog Drummond*. 1920; reprint, Holicong, PA: Wildside Press, 2014.

Menzies, Janet. *Children of the Doomed Voyage*. Chichester, UK: John Wiley & Sons, 2005.

Mulligan, Timothy P. *Neither Sharks nor Wolves: The Men of Nazi Germany's U-Boat Arm, 1939–1945*. Annapolis, MD: Naval Institute Press, 1999.

Nagorski, M. Bohdan. "Eight Days in a Lifeboat." With F. B. Czarnomski. In *They Fight for Poland: War in the First Person*, edited by F. B. Czarnomski. London: George Allen & Unwin, 1941.

Nagorski, Tom. *Miracles on the Water: The Heroic Survivors of a World War II U-Boat Attack*. New York: Hyperion, 2006.

Ondaatje, Michael. *The Cat's Table*. New York: Knopf, 2011.

Opie, Iona, and Peter Opie. *Children's Games in Street and Playground*. Oxford: Oxford University Press, 1970.

O'Sullivan, Rory. *Join the Navy? Get Torpedoed First!* Translated by Caroline Beaumont Ail. Annecy, France: self-published, June 2001. Original articles published in French in *Bulletin l'association des anciens élèves de Saint Michel d'Annecy*, 1982–87.

Shaffer, Mary Ann, and Annie Barrows. *The Guernsey Literary and Potato Peel Pie Society*. New York: Dial Press, 2008.

Shakespeare, Geoffrey. *Let Candles Be Brought In*. London: Macdonald, 1949.

*Smith, Lyn. *Young Voices: British Children Remember the Second World War*. With the Imperial War Museum. London: Viking, 2007.

*Struther, Jan. *Mrs. Miniver*. London: Chatto & Windus, 1939. Reprint, San Diego: Harcourt Brace Jovanovich, 1990.

Summers, Julie. *When the Children Came Home: Stories of Wartime Evacuees*. London: Simon & Schuster, 2011.

*Vadgama, Kusoom. *India in Britain: The Indian Contribution to the British Way of Life*. London: Robert Royce, 1984.

*Visram, Rozina. *Ayahs, Lascars and Princes: Indians in Britain 1700–1947*. London: Pluto Press, 1986.

Waters, Sarah. *The Night Watch*. New York: Penguin, 2006.

INTERVIEWS

Imperial War Museum (IWM). Sound Archive. London, iwm.org.uk.

- Derek Bech, Sept. 5, 2002
- Bess Walder Cummings, March 31, 2000
- Rolf Hilse, April 2004
- Jack Sidney Keeley, June 28, 2000
- Barbara Dagmar Partridge (née Bech), July 28, 2000

- Colin Ryder Richardson, Oct. 1, 2000
- Kenneth John Sparks, Sept. 27, 2001
- Harry Frederick Steels, Aug. 6, 2002
- Sonia Bech Williams, May 8, 2002

Merseyside Maritime Museum. City of Benares Collection. Liverpool, England, liverpoolmuseums.org.uk/maritime/collections/city-of-benares/. Interview number SA/7/104.

- Barbara Dagmar Partridge (née Bech), 2013
- Derek Bech, 2013

By author.
- John Baker. Via FaceTime, January 31, 2018; May 30–31, 2018; July 29, 2018; Derby, England.
- Sonia Bech Williams. Via phone, November 2, 2017. Via Skype, November 25, 2017. In person, May 25–30, 2018; Graffham, England.
- Maggie Paterson, In person, May 28, 2018; Heyshott, England.

DOCUMENTS

Bech, Barbara, Sonia Bech, and Derek Bech. *Childhood Memories of the Aldwick Bay Estate.* Sussex Riviera Millennium Supplement. Aldwick Bay Company Limited: 2000.

Bech, Derek. Personal statement: *The Story of Derek Bech, Aged 9, Survivor from 'City of Benares,'* no date.

Ellerman City Line Ltd. *City of Benares* Records. Glasgow University Archive Services, Scotland.

Imperial War Museum. Private Papers and Miscellaneous Documents. London, iwm.org.uk.

India office, British Library, London. Miscellaneous papers regarding lascars who died on the *City of Benares.*

The National Archives of the UK. Miscellaneous papers and documents concerning the *City of Benares.*

FILM, TELEVISION, AND RADIO

Documentaries

"Children of the Doomed Voyage." Produced and directed by Steve Humphries. *Timewatch.* Season 24, episode 11, aired Nov. 18, 2005, on BBC Two (UK), 50 mins.

" 'City of Benares' Survivors." News footage, British Pathe, 2:20 mins, britishpathe. com/video/city-of-benares-survivors.

Finest Hour: The Battle of Britain. Directed by Nick Read. Produced by WGBH, Brook Lapping Productions, and BBC. PBS Home Video, 2003. DVD, 220 mins.

The First Day of the Blitz. Directed by Nick Maddocks. Testimony Films, 2010. youtube.com/watch?v=KtZema1yjOk&t=5s, 60 mins.

"A Harrowing Journey Remembered." Michele Norris. All Things Considered, National Public Radio, May 12, 2006.

"Torpedoing of SS City of Benares." Eric Davis. BBC, Sept. 23, 1940.

U534: Silent Shadows. Picturewise Film and Cultex Media for Merseytravel, Liverpool, UK. Produced and edited by Stig Thornsohn and Henrik Laier, 2009. DVD, 53 mins.

World War II in Colour. Nugus/Martin Productions, 2009. Netflix, 13 episodes, 11 hrs, 5 mins.

Fictional Feature Films

Das Boot. Written and directed by Wolfgang Peterson. Bavaria Films, 1981.

Hope and Glory. Written and directed by John Boorman. Columbia Pictures, 1987.

Mrs. Miniver. Directed by William Wyler. Metro-Goldwyn-Mayer, 1942.

Titanic. Written and directed by James Cameron. Paramount Pictures, 1997.

NEWSPAPER ARTICLES AND WEBSITES

I read hundreds of newspaper articles and visited many websites over the course of researching and writing this book. They are too numerous to list here, though many are referenced in the endnotes. These are the newspaper sources and websites I used most.

Newspaper Article Sources

British Newspaper Archive, britishnewspaperarchive.co.uk/
JSTOR (Journal Storage), jstor.org
The New York Times archives, nytimes.com
ProQuest, proquest.com

Websites

Ancestry.com
BBC, BBC News, and BBC History for Kids: bbc.com, news.bbc.co.uk, and bbc
    .co.uk/history/forkids/
The British Pathé (for film footage of the *City of Benares* story, including films
    of the surviving children and Mary Cornish, like this one: britishpathe.com
    /video/city-of-benares-survivors)
The Imperial War Museum Collections online, iwm.org.uk/collections
Merseyside Maritime Museum, liverpoolmuseums.org.uk/maritime/index.aspx
MovieTone, movietone.com
The National Archives of the UK, nationalarchives.gov.uk
U-Boat.net, uboat.net/

For more information about my research process, visit DeborahHeiligman.com.

ENDNOTES

CHAPTER 1: *The Noise of War*

4. "Never in the field": Winston Churchill, speech, Aug. 20, 1940, *Parliamentary Debates*, Commons, 5th Series (1909–81), vol. 364, cols. 1159–71.

4. "to wage war": Winston Churchill, speech, May 13, 1940, *Parliamentary Debates*, Commons, 5th Series (1909–81), vol. 360, cols. 1501–2.

9. U-boat 48 had departed: Rolf Hilse, interview by Peter M. Hart, April 2004, Imperial War Museum, MP3 audio, 320 mins., iwm.org.uk/collections/item/object/80023889, reel 5.

9. emotionally charged opera: Bess Walder Cummings, interview by Lyn Smith, March 31, 2000, Imperial War Museum, MP3 audio, 140 mins.

12. pinched and worn: Eleanor B. Huxley, *Atlantic Ordeal: The Story of Mary Cornish* (New York: Harper & Brothers, 1942), p. 25.

13. Cockney bossiness: Ralph Barker, *Children of the Benares: A War Crime and Its Victims* (London: Methuen, 1987), p. 6.

CHAPTER 2: *Sailing to Safety*

14. It had been a hot: Meteorological Office, "September, 1940," *Monthly Weather Report* 57, no. 9, metoffice.gov.uk/binaries/content/assets/mohippo/pdf/j/4/sep1940.pdf.

16. specific packing list: Children's Overseas Reception Board, packing list, Imperial War Museum.

19. He had turned nine: Jack Keeley birth certificate, July 21, 1931.

20. "When things go wrong": Geoffrey Shakespeare, *Let Candles Be Brought In* (London: Macdonald, 1949), p. 257.

20. "Stop it at once": Shakespeare, p. 257.

20. He'd seen the newsreels: Jack Sidney Keeley, interview by Lyn Smith, June 28, 2000, Imperial War Museum,

MP3 audio, 90 mins., iwm.org.uk/collections/item/object/80019131.

21. Those scared the life: Jack Sidney Keeley, IWM interview, June 28, 2000.

22. He bravely agreed: Colin Ryder Richardson, interview in "Children of the Doomed Voyage," produced and directed by Steve Humphries, *Timewatch*, season 24, episode 11, BBC Two (UK), Nov. 18, 2005.

22. Colin didn't know this: Julian Ryder Richardson, email to author, Oct. 26, 2018.

23. We'll have a grand time: Tom Nagorski, *Miracles on the Water: The Heroic Survivors of a World War II U-Boat Attack* (New York: Hyperion, 2006), p. 91.

23. "A British evacuee ship": Reuters, "Children's Ship Torpedoed: All Passengers Saved," *Times of India*, Sept. 2, 1940.

24. The article did not report: Shakespeare, p. 271.

24. "everyone had swimming pools": Jack Sidney Keeley, IWM interview, June 28, 2000.

CHAPTER 3: *A Floating Palace*

25. "We had our photo taken": Barker, p. 13.

28. "We should illuminate": John McGovern, debate of Children's Overseas Reception Scheme, July 2, 1940, *Parliamentary Debates*, Commons, 5th Series (1909–81), vol. 362, col. 753.

29. Fred's parents had already suffered: Harry Frederick Steels, interview by Lyn Smith, Aug. 6, 2002, Imperial War Museum, MP3 audio, 60 mins., iwm.org.uk/collections/item/object/80022267.

29. Here y'are, nippy: Harry Frederick Steels, IWM interview, Aug. 6, 2002.

29. Fred thought: Harry Frederick Steels, IWM interview, Aug. 6, 2002;

and interview in "Children of the Doomed Voyage," *Timewatch*.

29. The ship had forty-three: Barker, p. 161.

30. "We have got plenty of dark men": "Homeless—Lose Five," *Daily Mirror* (London), Sept. 23, 1940.

30. "Indian stewards": Bess Walder Cummings, IWM interview, March 31, 2000.

31. "Eddie and Lennie": This and following quote from Gussie's letter are from "Homeless—Lose Five," *Daily Mirror* (London), Sept. 23, 1940.

34. He witnessed so many crashes: Sonia Bech Williams, author interview via Skype, Nov. 25, 2017.

34. What have you got: Derek Bech, interview by Lyn Smith, Sept. 5, 2002, Imperial War Museum, audiocassette, 120 mins.

34. his tabby cat, Tim: Sonia Bech Williams, author interview via Skype, Nov. 25, 2017.

35. He even had a little suitcase: Sonia Bech Williams, author interview via Skype, Nov. 25, 2017.

35. "We shall fight": Winston Churchill, speech, June 4, 1940, *Parliamentary Debates*, Commons, 5th Series (1909–81), vol. 361, cols. 787–796.

35. Barbara could see: Barbara Dagmar Partridge (née Bech), interview by Lyn Smith, July 27, 2000, Imperial War Museum, MP3 audio, 110 mins., iwm.org.uk/collections/item/object/80019217.

36. that was when: John McGlashan (second engineer), report, Sept. 30, 1940, *City of Benares*, Records of Ellerman City Line Ltd., 1901–1970s, UGD 131/1, Glasgow University Archive Services, Scotland.

CHAPTER 4: *Desserts and Drills*

38. "It is very lovely": All quotes from Gussie's letter come from Barker, pp. 13–14.

38. it was worth it!: Kenneth John Sparks, interview by Lyn Smith, Sept. 27, 2001, Imperial War Museum,

MP3 audio, 80 mins., iwm.org.uk/collections/item/object/80020747.

38. The cooks and waiters . . . cherry sauce: Ellerman Lines, Glasgow Archives, *S.S. City of Benares—cruise*, no date.

39. "We go into a big room": "Homeless—Lose Five," *Daily Mirror* (London), Sept. 23, 1940.

39. She hadn't seen a banana: Bess Walder Cummings, IWM interview, March 31, 2000.

39. Sonia was charmed: Sonia Bech Williams, author interview via Skype, Nov. 25, 2017.

40. For Jack Keeley: Jack Sidney Keeley, IWM interview, June 28, 2000.

40. "We have a play room": Violet's and Gussie's letters are in Barker, p. 14.

40. There was a Noah's ark: Ellerman City Line Ltd., promotional brochures, ca. 1936, *City of Benares*, Records of Ellerman City Line Ltd., 1901–1970s, UGD 131/1, Glasgow University Archive Services, Scotland.

41. library's windows: Barbara Dagmar Partridge (née Bech), IWM interview, July 27, 2000.

41. The ship had twelve lifeboats: "Minute Sheet" for *City of Benares*, Evacuation of Children. From the National Archives UK.

42. "EMERGENCY ARRANGEMENTS": Ellerman City Line Ltd., documents of *City of Benares*, 1940, Records of Ellerman City Line Ltd., 1901–1970s, UGD 131/1, Glasgow University Archive Services, Scotland.

44. The first lifeboat drill: McGlashan, report, Sept. 30, 1940.

44. "Me, Gussie and Violet": Barker, p. 14; and "Homeless—Lose Five," *Daily Mirror* (London), Sept. 23, 1940.

44. Sonia got an immediate crush: Sonia Bech Williams, interview by Lyn Smith, May 8, 2002, Imperial War Museum, MP3 audio, 120 mins., iwm.org.uk/collections/item/object/80021858; and Sonia Bech Williams, author interview via phone, Nov. 2, 2017.

44. There were ten children: Barker, p. 10; Tom Nagorski, p. 38.

44. "in case our boat got hit": This and following quotes from Gussie's letter are from "Homeless—Lose Five," *Daily Mirror* (London), Sept. 23, 1940.

CHAPTER 5: *Wish Me Luck as You Wave Me Goodbye*

46. lead ship in a convoy: "Life on Board for the Children," *City of Benares* Collection, Merseyside Maritime Museum, liverpoolmuseums.org.uk/maritime/collections/city-of-benares/life-on-board.aspx; "'City of Benares' (1936)", Glasgow University Archive Services, Scotland.

46. the Flower class corvettes: Don Kindell, "OB.213," OB Convoy Series, Arnold Hague Convoy Database, convoyweb.org.uk/ob2/index.html.

47. When Mrs. Bech heard: Sonia Bech Williams, IWM interview, May 8, 2002.

47. Derek Bech had noticed: Derek Bech, IWM interview, Sept. 5, 2002; Sonia Bech Williams, author interview via Skype, Nov. 25, 2017

47. It had 215 crew members: Tom Nagorski, p. 5; Barker, p. 161.

48. Their favorite songs: Shakespeare, p. 259; "There'll Always Be an England," words and music by Ross Parker and Hughie Charles, 1939, Dash Music Company Ltd.; "Wish Me Luck (as You Wave Me Goodbye)," words by Phil Park, music by Harry Parr-Davies, 1939, Chappell Music Ltd.

49. There had been a gale: Meteorological Office, "September, 1940."

49. The German war submarine: Rolf Hilse, IWM interview by Peter M. Hart, April 2004.

50. Michael Rennie, twenty-three: Portrait of Michael Rennie from various sources, especially an obituary in the November 1940 edition of *The Blue*, a publication of his secondary school, Christ's Hospital; a brief mention of him in a 1935 edition; and letters and memories published in the Michaelmas and Summer 1995 editions. Obituary by Barclay Hankin, remembrance and letter by his friend Dr. J. R. Purser.

53. one boy knew: Huxley, pp. 21–22.

54. Johnny Baker got a reputation: John Baker, author interviews via FaceTime, Jan. 31, 2018, and May 30–31, 2018.

56. Sometimes Colin would wander: Colin Ryder Richardson, interview by Lyn Smith, Oct. 1, 2000, Imperial War Museum, MP3 audio, 140 mins., iwm.org.uk/collections/item/object/80019493.

56. Colin invented a game: Colin Ryder Richardson, IWM interview, Oct. 1, 2000.

56. Derek Bech watched: Derek Bech, IWM interview, Sept. 5, 2002.

CHAPTER 6: *Secrets at Sea*

60. I'd as soon put: This and preceding paragraph are from Tom Nagorski, p. 51.

CHAPTER 7: *U-boat 48*

63. His submarine, U-48: Specifics of VIIB type submarines and U-48 in particular can be found at Gudmundur Helgason, ed., "Type VIIB" and "U-48," uboat.net.

64. In its two years of active service: Timothy P. Mulligan, *Neither Sharks nor Wolves: The Men of Nazi Germany's U-Boat Arm, 1939–1945* (Annapolis, MD: Naval Institute Press, 1999), p. 142.

64. Good morning, Captain: Rolf Hilse, IWM interview, April 2004.

65. Admiral Karl Dönitz: Mulligan, p. 35.

66. "bored sick": Rolf Hilse, IWM interview, April 2004.

67. Rolf Hilse actually met: Rolf Hilse, IWM interview, April 2004.

CHAPTER 8: *September 17, 1940*

70. Derek Bech stayed in bed: Derek Bech, IWM interview, Sept. 5, 2002.

71. Louis came over: Bess Walder Cummings, IWM interview, March 31, 2000; Bess Walder to Miss Simonis, Oct. 1, 1940, private papers of B. Walder, Imperial War Museum.

71. "cut and run for it": Tom Nagorski, p. 61; Barker p. 20.

73. In her group Mary: Huxley, pp. 16–17.

74. And in 119 seconds: Rolf Hilse, IWM interview, April 2004.

74. Just as Mary: Huxley, p. 25.

CHAPTER 9: *It's Only a Torpedo*

76. Some children were killed: Some accounts say one or two; others, dozens. Most of the deaths would come later.

78. He knew exactly: Jack Sidney Keeley, IWM interview, June 28, 2000.

78. He woke up one: Janet Menzies, *Children of the Doomed Voyage* (Chichester, UK: John Wiley & Sons, 2005), p. 87; Harry Frederick Steels, IWM interview, Aug. 6, 2002; and his interview in "Children of the Doomed Voyage," *Timewatch*.

80. At 10:05, the freighter's bridge: "Ex: Marina," unsigned report (14241), probably from the first officer of the SS *Marina* in 1941, Imperial War Museum.

80. the *Benares* was over: The 1940 *Lloyd's Register of Ships* lists the *City of Benares* at 11,081 tons. The U-48 crew estimated it at 11,800 per Rolf Hilse, IWM interview, April 2004.

80. A few of the crew: Rolf Hilse, IWM interview, April 2004.

80. "We watched the lifeboats": Menzies, p. 74; Rolf Hilse, IWM interview, April 2004.

81. The sick escort: Rory O'Sullivan, *Join the Navy? Get Torpedoed First*, trans. Caroline Beaumont Ail (Annecy, France: self-published, 2001), p. 25.

85. Mrs. Walder had come home: Bess Walder Cummings, IWM interview, March 31, 2000.

85. But when Bess went back: Bess Walder to Miss Simonis, Oct. 1, 1940, Imperial War Museum.

85. In the time it took her: Scene is reconstructed from Bess's letter to Miss Simonis, Oct. 1, 1940, IWM; and Bess Walder Cummings, IWM interview, March 31, 2000; as well as other accounts.

86. "his devotion to duty": Senior surviving officer report, Oct. 8, 1940, S.S. "City of Benares," Records of Ellerman City Line Ltd., Glasgow University Archive Services, Scotland.

87. the *Winchelsea* had rescued: Helgason, "Crown Arun," Ships Hit by U-boats in WWII, uboat.net/allies/merchants/ships/528.html; Kindell, "HX.71," HX Convoy Series, Arnold Hague Convoy Database.

87. at maximum speed: The maximum speed of the H-Class destroyer was thirty-six knots. M. J. Whitley, *Destroyers of World War Two: An International Encyclopedia* (Annapolis, MD: 1988), p. 111.

87. "One for us": *Liverpool Echo*, Sept. 13, 1965.

88. HELP! Bess yelled: The following scene is reconstructed from Tom Nagorski, p. 73; Menzies, p. 104; Walder to Simonis, Oct. 1, 1940, IWM; Bess Walder Cummings, IWM interview, March 31, 2000; and Bess Walder Cummings, interview in "Children of the Doomed Voyage," *Timewatch*.

89. Mary Cornish was still making: Huxley, p. 26–28.

CHAPTER 10: *Fate's Hand*

94. Were we thankful?: Walder to Simonis, Oct. 1, 1940, IWM.

95. We'll be picked up: Barker, p. 58.

95. Although the ship's stokers: Thanks for this explanation goes to Jennifer Robertson, assistant curator of maritime history at the Merseyside Maritime Museum in Liverpool.

97. Fred saw chaos: Harry Frederick Steels, IWM interview, Aug. 6, 2002.

98. Mary Cornish stood: Huxley, p. 27.

98. "I've just been through there": Huxley, p. 28.

CHAPTER 11: *The Middle of the Atlantic*

102. It all happened very quickly: John Baker, author interviews via FaceTime, Jan. 31, 2018, May 30–31, 2018.

103. After the disaster: John Baker, author interviews via FaceTime, Jan. 31, 2018, May 30–31, 2018; Menzies, pp. 94–95.

103. Marjorie Day: Barker, p. 63.

107. "The unique advantage": I.R. Fleming & Co, advertisement posted at the Merseyside Maritime Museum, Liverpool, England.

108. Yes, the Fleming gear took: Barker, pp. 9–10; Michael H. Standart, reply to "Mauretania II Lifeboat," Encyclopedia Titanica forum, Nov. 19, 2007, encyclopedia-titanica.org/community/threads/mauretania-iilifeboat.25076/.

108. Beth Cummings was one: "I Survived the Massacre of 77 Children," *North Wales Daily Post*, Sept. 6, 2004, dailypost.co.uk/news/northwales-news/survived-massacre-77-children-2922925.

CHAPTER 12: *The Lounge*

111. bought those blue pajamas: Sonia Bech Williams, author interview via Skype, Nov. 25, 2017.

113. Over his pajamas: Derek Bech, IWM interview, Sept. 5, 2002; Sonia Bech Williams, IWM interview, May 8, 2002; and Barbara Dagmar Partridge (née Bech), IWM interview, July 27, 2000.

116. Go to your boat stations!: Barbara Dagmar Partridge (née Bech), IWM interview, July 27, 2000.

116. Barbara looked at the rope: Barbara Dagmar Partridge (née Bech), IWM interview, July 27, 2000.

120. "Women and children first": Colin Ryder Richardson, IWM interview, Oct. 1, 2000.

120. Laszlo went off: Tom Nagorski, p. 110; Barker, p. 66.

CHAPTER 13: *A Long Green Tunnel*

128. Someone was calling out. Sonia Bech Williams, author interview, May 28, 2018.

129. "grabbed on to a little piece": Eric Davis in "Torpedoing of SS *City of Benares*," BBC recording, Sept. 23, 1940, 7 mins., Imperial War Museum.

129. All around him, he could hear: Jack Sidney Keeley, IWM interview, June 28, 2000.

CHAPTER 14: *Ships Cry*

134. The commodore: Colin Brown McDonald (supernumerary chief

engineer), report, Sept. 27, 1940, Glasgow Archives.

134. Fred kept his eye: Harry Frederick Steels, IWM interview, Aug. 6, 2002.

134. Mary Cornish watched: Huxley, p. 31.

136. a rush of water and noise: Colin Ryder Richardson, IWM interview, Oct. 1, 2000.

136. She thought, I don't believe: Barbara Dagmar Partridge (née Bech), IWM interview, July 27, 2000.

137. Later a sailor asked Bess: Bess Walder Cummings, IWM interview, March 31, 2000; Michele Norris, "A Harrowing Journey Remembered," May 12, 2006, All Things Considered, National Public Radio.

CHAPTER 15: *The Longest Night*

138. Five people were Derek Bech, IWM interview, Sept. 5, 2002; Sonia Bech Williams, IWM interview, May 8, 2002; and "In the Water," Merseyside Maritime Museum, liverpoolmuseums.org.uk/maritime/collections/city-of-benares/in-the-water.aspx.

138. Milligan was nineteen: Milligan says he was nineteen, but he might have been only seventeen, according to Sonia Bech Williams, author interview in person, May 28, 2018.

138. They had had five minutes: Newspaper reports received from Tommy Milligan, private collection of Sonia Bech Williams.

140. For much of the time: Sonia Bech Williams, author interview via phone, Nov. 2, 2017.

140. Colin figured: Colin Ryder Richardson, IWM interview, Oct. 1, 2000.

141. Colin had never seen: Julian Ryder-Richardson, email message to author, Aug. 12, 2018.

141. At some point he put his hands: Tom Nagorski, p. 123; Barker, p. 83.

141. The farm at Glan Usk near Abergavenny: Julian Ryder-Richardson, email message to author, July 18, 2018; Colin Ryder Richardson, IWM interview, Oct. 1, 2000.

142. Jack Keeley couldn't stop: Eric Davis, "Torpedoing of SS *City of Benares*," BBC; Jack Sidney Keeley, IWM interview, June 28, 2000.

144. It was John McGlashan: McGlashan's actions after the torpedo struck and his experiences on the raft are from his report to the Ellerman City Line Ltd., Sept. 30, 1940.

147. She was riveted with fright: Sonia Bech Williams, author interview in person, May 28, 2018; Eric Davis, "Torpedoing of SS *City of Benares*," BBC.

148. In a matter of hours: Bess Walder to Miss Simonis, Oct. 1, 1940; Bess Walder, IWM interview, March 31, 2000.

149. She woke up under the water: Sonia Bech Williams, IWM interview, May 8, 2002.

152. Mister! Jack said: Jack Sidney Keeley, IWM interview, June 28, 2000.

CHAPTER 16: *Break of Day*

154. Sir, he asked Eric: Jack and Eric Davis's conversation is from "Torpedoing of SS *City of Benares*," BBC; Barker, p. 101.

155. It was, Bess thought: Bess Walder to Miss Simonis, Oct. 1, 1940.

157. Down in the trough: Colin Ryder Richardson, interview, Oct. 1, 2000.

157. The gloves his mother had put: Sarah Ryder-Richardson, email message to author, July 18, 2018.

160. She thought it was disgusting: Sonia Bech Williams, author interview via Skype, Nov. 25, 2017.

CHAPTER 17: *Best Possible Speed*

162. fifteen knots (about seventeen miles per hour): A knot is 1 nautical mile per hour, and a nautical mile is 1,852 meters, or 1.15 land miles.

163. about one in the afternoon: Tom Nagorski, p. 151.

166. The Bechs saw its silver . . . where they fell fast asleep: The account of the Bechs' rescue by the *Hurricane* is from Derek Bech, IWM interview, Sept. 5, 2002; and Sonia Bech Williams, IWM interview, May 8, 2002.

169. It took half an hour: Tom Nagorski p. 153; Barker, p. 104.

CHAPTER 18: *The* Hurricane

170. Bess and Beth were: Bess Walder Cummings, IWM interview, March 31, 2000.

171. How do you stop: Barker, p. 102; Tom Nagorski, p. 147.

172. *There's something quite exciting*: Hugh Crofton Simms, "City of Benares," *HMS* Hurricane *at Sea*, Sept. 27, 1940, Glasgow University Archive Services, Scotland.

172. Perhaps, Jack thought: Jack Sidney Keeley, IWM interview, June 28, 2000.

173. Jack and Eric shouted: Jack Sidney Keeley, IWM interview, June 28, 2000.

175. "I was by this time": McGlashan, report, Sept. 30, 1940.

175. "all that was free": Eric Davis, "Torpedoing of SS *City of Benares*," BBC recording, Sept. 27, 1940, 2 mins.

176. "was like walking out": Jack Sidney Keeley, IWM interview, June 28, 2000.

176. *There's something very terrible*: Hugh Crofton Simms, "City of Benares," *HMS* Hurricane *at Sea*, Sept. 27, 1940, Glasgow University Archive Services, Scotland.

177. Then she saw masts: Bess Walder to Miss Simonis, Oct. 1, 1940.

181. Please, God, let them live: Tom Nagorski, p. 161.

182. But Colin couldn't move: Colin Ryder Richardson, IWM interview, Oct. 1, 2000.

185. Monika and her husband: "Travelers from England and Scotland Arrive on the Cameronia," *The New York Times*, Oct. 29, 1940, p. 32.

CHAPTER 19: *Phoenixes*

188. Thank goodness for that: Barbara Dagmar Partridge (née Bech), IWM interview, July 27, 2000.

192. "There are still children": Michael Rennie's actions are recounted in Louis Walder's letter to the Reverend William Maxwell Rennie, Oct. or Nov.

1940, collection of St. Jude on the Hill, London, typed transcription, blog.nationalarchives.gov.uk/blog/remembering-city-benares-tragedy/corb4/#.

193. Everyone on the boat: "Statement by W. J. Lee, 3rd Officer, *City of Benares*," Sept. 20, 1940, Glasgow University Archive Services, Scotland.

194. "Just how fortunate": Bess Walder Cummings, IWM interview, March 31, 2000.

CHAPTER 20: *"In Spite of All the Precautions"*

198. I am very distressed: Geoffrey Shakespeare to Tom Myatt, Sept. 19, 1940, private papers of Miss Beryl Myatt, Imperial War Museum, London.

199. "We were expecting a cablegram": "Eight Children Went—1 Lives," *Daily Mirror* (London), Sept. 23, 1940, in private papers of Sonia Bech Williams, Graffham, England.

201. Vicar had a mural painted: Michaelmas edition of *The Blue*, Dr. J. R. Purser, 1995.

201. Mary Cornish's younger sister: Maggie Paterson (Eileen Paterson's daughter-in-law), author interview in person, May 28, 2018.

CHAPTER 21: *Lifeboat 12*

202. He'd been asleep: Ron Cooper (fourth officer), report, Sept. 29, 1940, *City of Benares*, Records of Ellerman City Line Ltd., 1901–1970s, UGD 131/1, Glasgow University Archive Services, Scotland.

202. Six CORB boys: Huxley, p. 28.

202. "in case any stragglers": Cooper, report, Sept. 29, 1940.

203. He ordered the four: Huxley, p. 30; M. Bohdan Nagorski, "Eight Days in a Lifeboat," p. 202–3.

203. So after a great deal: Derek Capel, interview in "Children of the Doomed Voyage," *Timewatch*.

203. For Fred Steels: Harry Frederick Steels, IWM interview, Aug. 6, 2002.

204. Just as they were getting clear: Cooper, report, Sept. 29, 1940.

204. Upon hearing that: Cooper, report, Sept. 29, 1940.

205. He especially loved the desserts: Kenneth John Sparks, IWM interview, Sept. 27, 2001.

206. My mum'll kill me: Menzies, p. 77.

206. supposed to be number 8: Menzies, p. 90.

206. a thin silk blouse: Mary Cornish's condition in the lifeboat is from Huxley, p. 32.

207. He was the managing director: Nagorski was managing director of the Gdynia-America Steamship Company. M. Bohdan Nagorski, p. 198.

208. On that first day: Cooper, report, Sept. 29, 1940.

209. a ship's biscuit with a sardine: Huxley, p. 37; Menzies, p. 155

209. first to the children: M. Bohdan Nagorski, pp. 205–6.

210. When he came to: O'Sullivan, p. 29.

CHAPTER 22: *I Spy Nothing*

213. On days without school: John Baker, author interviews via FaceTime, Jan. 31, 2018, May 30–31, 2018.

213. They'd play running and chasing games: Iona Opie and Peter Opie, *Children's Games in Street and Playground* (Oxford: Oxford University Press, 1970); and Jane Weller and Irene Weller, in conversation with the editor.

214. "Run rabbit, run rabbit": "Run, Rabbit, Run," words by Noel Gay and Ralph Butler, music by Noel Gay, 1939, Noel Gray Music Co. Ltd.

216. A very few sea birds: Huxley, p. 50.

217. "Demobilised officer": This and the following Drummond quote are from Cyril McNeile, *Bull-Dog Drummond* (1920; reprint, Holicong, PA: Wildside Press, 2014), pp. 27, 84.

218. Mary had Bulldog Drummond: Huxley, p. 51.

CHAPTER 23: *Perils at Sea*

220. He told them: O'Sullivan, p. 27.

221. He'd swim around: Barker, p. 128.

221. He's a proper screwball: Menzies, p. 164.

221. He seemed to have a knack: Huxley, p. 57.

221. A few times he was personally nasty: Huxley, pp. 58–59.

222. "Any old iron": "Any Old Iron," words by Fred Terry and A. E. Sheppard, music by Charles Collins, 1911, Herman Darewski Music Publishing Co.

222. Bohdan Nagorski thought: Barker, p. 138.

223. Father Rory admired his expertise: This and other observations about Critchley are from Rory O'Sullivan to Doug Critchley, Nov. 2, 1940, Maritime Archive, DX/2165, Merseyside Maritime Museum, Liverpool.

CHAPTER 24: *British Heroes Don't Snivel*

225. "crisp sausages": John Buchan, *The Thirty-Nine Steps* (1915; reprint, Boston: Houghton Mifflin, 1943), pp. 59–60.

226. They were so hard: Harry Frederick Steels, IWM interview, Aug. 6, 2002.

226. They dreamed of sausages: Menzies, p. 158.

226. For a few moments: Huxley, p. 49.

227. British heroes don't snivel: Huxely, p. 54.

CHAPTER 25: *Hope Is a Fine Feather of Smoke*

228. But now, around four o'clock: Cooper, report, Sept. 29, 1940.

228. As the dot grew larger: Huxley, p. 63.

228. Nagorski had crawled: M. Bohdan Nagorski, p. 212.

229. Mary Cornish's petticoat: This and Mary Cornish's dream are from Huxley, pp. 63–64.

229. Father Rory could see: O'Sullivan, p. 32.

229. Cooper and his crew: Huxley, p. 65; M. Bohdan Nagorski, p. 212.

230. Cooper explained how: O'Sullivan, p. 32.

230. Mary exulted: Huxley, p. 65.

230. "'Hope' is the thing with feathers": Emily Dickinson, *The Complete Poems of Emily Dickinson*, ed. Thomas H. Johnson (Boston: Little, Brown, 1960), p. 116.

CHAPTER 26: *Darkest Hours*

232. For the first time: M. Bohdan Nagorski, p. 213; O'Sullivan, p. 32; Huxley, pp. 64–68.

234. "Mary was loved": This and the following excerpts from condolence letters to Eileen Paterson come from, in order of appearance in text, Vera S. Ayton, Sept. 23, 1940; Fanny (last name not readable), Sept. 26, 1940; Ann Bourne, Sept. 24, 1940; name not readable (possibly Overton), Sept. 25, 1940; Lara Boyle, Sept. 22, 1940; Phoebe (no last name), Sept. 23, 1940; Phyllis (no last name), Sept. 23, 1940; private collection of Maggie Paterson.

236. At least one shipwrecked: Gabriel García Márquez, *Shipwrecked Sailor*, trans. Randolph Hogan (New York: Knopf, 1986), pp. 38, 44.

CHAPTER 27: *Illusions, Delusions, More Nightmares*

240. It made him feel good to be of use: M. Bohdan Nagorski, p. 214.

241. I'm mad, I'm mad: Huxley, p. 74.

243. When the sun rose: Huxley, pp. 75–76.

CHAPTER 28: *And on the Eighth Day . . .*

246. The seaplane signaled a Morse code: Tom Nagorski, p. 266.

246. "The plane dropped": Cooper, report, Sept. 29, 1940.

246. Low on fuel: James MacDonald, "46 of the *Benares* Saved After 8 days," *The New York Times*, Sept. 27, 1940.

247. "draining every drop": Huxley, p. 79.

247. "I flew across": MacDonald, "46 of the *Benares* Saved After 8 days."

251. "Mummy, I haven't got Peter for you": Barker, p. 137; Tom Nagorski, p. 286.

251. he never hugged anyone: Heather Greenaway, "I've Not Hugged Anyone for 71 Years," *Daily Record*, Sept. 5, 2011.

CHAPTER 29: *A Watery Grave*

253. "This is not war". "Father of 5 Victims Joins Up Again," *Daily Telegraph* (London), Sept. 23, 1940, in private papers of Sonia Bech Williams; Tom Nagorski, p. 318.

254. The *Nova Scotia* passengers: Jennifer Robertson, "The City of Benares Legacy 75 Years On," blog, Merseyside Maritime Museum, Oct. 20, 2015, blog.liverpoolmuseums.org .uk/2015/10/the-city-of-benares-legacy-75-years-on/; Michael Fethney, *The Absurd and the Brave: CORB—The True Account of the British Government's World War II Evacuation of Children Overseas* (Sussex, UK: Book Guild, 2000), p. 156.

255. Alan Francis: Alan Francis's story is compiled from the film *Finest Hour: The Battle of Britain*, 2003; Tim Clayton and Phil Craig, *Finest Hour: The Battle of Britain* (New York: Touchstone), pp. 241, 257–8, 267–9, 286–7; Alan Francis, "War Through the Eyes of a Wembley Schoolboy," WW2 People's War, BBC, Aug. 8, 2004, bbc.co.uk/history/ ww2peopleswar/stories/38/a2902538. shtml; Malin Lundin, "Alan Francis: Recollections of Life on the Home Front and the Cruelty of War," Memories of War, June 7, 2012, memoriesofwar.org .uk/page_id_228.aspx.

256. "Dear Sirs, . . . owing to the tragic": Mary and Robert Dixon to Ellerman City Line, Nov. 13, 1940, *City of Benares*, Records of Ellerman City Line Ltd., 1901–1970s, UGD 131/1, Glasgow University Archive Services, Scotland.

256. "Somewhere in England": Maureen Dixon, postcard to Mary and Robert Dixon, n.d., in Tony Henderson, "Sunderland Victims of Wartime Liner Sinking to Be Remembered at Memorial Service," Oct. 1, 2015, *Chronicle Live*, chroniclelive.co.uk/news/

north-eastnews/sunderland-victims-wartimeliner-sinking-10175356.

256. "Dear Sirs, . . . Excuse": George Crawford to Ellerman City Line, Oct. 18, 1940, *City of Benares*, Records of Ellerman City Line Ltd., 1901–1970s, UGD 131/1, Glasgow University Archive Services, Scotland

257. "As you will most probably be aware": Eleanor Wright to Ellerman Lines, Nov. 12, 1940.

258. Much later, long after: Julie Summers, *When the Children Came Home: Stories of Wartime Evacuees* (London: Simon & Schuster, 2011), p. 195; Jessica Mann, *Out of Harm's Way: The Wartime Evacuation of Children from Britain* (London: Headline, 2005), p. 320.

258. "You will have to think": Elspeth Davies to Mrs. Myatt, Oct. 2?, 1940, private papers of Beryl Myatt, Imperial War Museum.

260. These names are transliterated and so may not be consistent with other sources, such as India office papers and the Glasgow Archives. I chose the spellings listed on u.boat.net since that is most available to the reader.

INDEX